T0319001

Cambridge Elements ☰

Elements in the Philosophy of Religion
edited by
Yujin Nagasawa
University of Birmingham

THE PROBLEM OF EVIL

Michael Tooley
University of Colorado Boulder

CAMBRIDGE
UNIVERSITY PRESS

CAMBRIDGE
UNIVERSITY PRESS

University Printing House, Cambridge CB2 8BS, United Kingdom

One Liberty Plaza, 20th Floor, New York, NY 10006, USA

477 Williamstown Road, Port Melbourne, VIC 3207, Australia

314–321, 3rd Floor, Plot 3, Splendor Forum, Jasola District Centre, New Delhi – 110025, India

79 Anson Road, #06–04/06, Singapore 079906

Cambridge University Press is part of the University of Cambridge.

It furthers the University's mission by disseminating knowledge in the pursuit of education, learning, and research at the highest international levels of excellence.

www.cambridge.org
Information on this title: www.cambridge.org/9781108749053
DOI: 10.1017/9781108782029

First published 2019

A catalogue record for this publication is available from the British Library.

ISBN 978-1-108-74905-3 Paperback
ISSN 2399-5165 (online)
ISSN 2515-9763 (print)

The Problem of Evil

Elements in the Philosophy of Religion

DOI: 10.1017/9781108782029
First published online: August 2019

Michael Tooley
University of Colorado Boulder

Author for correspondence: Michael Tooley, michael.tooley.7@gmail.com

Abstract: Section 1 addresses issues that are important to think about in formulating arguments from evil. Section 2 is concerned with the question of how an incompatibility argument from evil is best formulated, and with possible responses to such arguments. Section 3 focuses on skeptical theism and on the work that skeptical theists need to do if they are to defend their claim of having defeated incompatibility versions of the argument from evil. Finally, Section 4 discusses evidential arguments from evil, and four different kinds of evidential argument are set out and critically examined.

Keywords: problem of evil, arguments from evil, incompatibility arguments, evidential arguments

ISBNs: 9781108749053 (PB), 9781108782029 (OC)
ISSNs: 2399-5165 (online), 2515-9763 (print)

Contents

Introduction and Overview

The Scope of the Problem of Evil and of Arguments from Evil: Relevant Conceptions of God

The term 'God' is used in many ways. Sometimes it is given a purely meta-physical interpretation, involving no moral properties: God is a prime mover, or the first cause, or a necessary being having its necessity of itself, or the ground of being, or a being whose essence is identical with its existence. Or God is not one being among other beings – even a supremely great being – but instead God is being itself. Or God is an ultimate reality to which no concepts truly apply.

Thus interpreted, no problem of evil arises: since such purely metaphysical definitions involve no moral concepts, the existence of such a being would not pose any puzzle concerning the existence of evil.

In sharp contrast are interpretations of the term 'God' that render appropriate certain religious attitudes, such as that of worship, or that connect up with important human hopes and desires – such as the desire that biological death not be the end of a person's existence, or the desire that, ultimately, justice will prevail, that good will triumph over evil. For what kind of being would make it reasonable to believe that such important desires are not in vain? Or what type of being would be worthy of worship?

A natural and very common answer is, first, that it must be disposed to care about the well-being of persons, and so, presumably, itself be a person. Secondly, it must be very powerful, to enable human persons to survive biological death, and to ensure that justice will ultimately exist. Thirdly, it must be very knowledgeable, to be aware of evils that should be eliminated or prevented. Finally, it must be at least basically moral rather than either evil or morally indifferent to the existence of evil.

Ideally, it would possess those properties in the highest degree. Thus one has classical theism's concept of God, according to which God is an omnipotent, omniscient, and morally perfect good person. It is then puzzling, however, why the world contains such an enormous number of horrendous evils. It is thus this classical conception of God that is most threatened by the problem of evil.

Consequently, some philosophers, theologians, and religious thinkers have proposed shifting to belief in a more limited deity – one that is not omnipotent or not omniscient. This, however, is not sufficient, as becomes clear when one asks *how limited* such a deity must be for evil not to pose a problem, since it would seem that such a being must be unable either to prevent or to eliminate the enormous ills that human flesh is heir to, including the suffering inflicted by other persons, or else it must lack all knowledge of such evils. Either way, a deity thus limited would provide no grounds for thinking, for example, that

humans survive biological death, or for hoping that, in the end, justice will
prevail.

What if, instead, one uses the term 'God' to refer to a being that is less than
morally perfect? The answer is that this seems even less satisfactory. For, first,
many of the great evils the world contains could be eliminated, or prevented, by
a being only moderately more powerful than humans; secondly, a being no more
knowledgeable than humans would know of their existence; and, thirdly, even a
moderately good human being, given the power to do so, would presumably
eliminate those evils. Conceiving of God as less than morally perfect provides
no escape, then, from the problem of evil.

What if, instead, one uses the term 'God' to mean simply an intelligent
creator of the universe, to whom no moral nature at all is ascribed? That
certainly enables one to escape the problem of evil, but such a creator is hardly
worthy of worship, nor would it provide any grounds for thinking human hopes
and desires concerning justice or survival of death will be met. One can attempt
to offer reasons for thinking that such an intelligent creator would also be
morally good, but then one is back on a collision course with the problem of
evil.

Finally, some religious thinkers have suggested that the idea of a *personal*
deity should be jettisoned: the term 'God' should be used instead for a completely impersonal force moving events toward what is good rather than what is
bad.

This is a perfectly coherent concept, but now questions arise as to how
strongly this force pushes events toward the good rather than the bad, how
accurate the 'information' is that determines how the force is directed, and how
powerful that force is. The stronger the force is in these respects, the more the
problem of evil will bear upon the existence of such an impersonal entity. An
impersonal God, in short, is as much exposed to the problem of evil as is the
personal God of classical theism.

Incompatibility Arguments versus Evidential Arguments

Any argument from evil starts with the claim either that the world contains
states of affairs that are intrinsically bad, in the sense of being intrinsically
undesirable, or, alternatively, that there are states of affairs that one should
prevent or eliminate if one knows of their existence and has the power to prevent
or eliminate them. A crucial question then arises, however, concerning what one
is attempting to prove, and here there are two alternatives. First, there are
incompatibility versions of the argument from evil, which attempt to demon-
strate that there are facts that *logically entail* that a deity of a certain sort does

not exist. Such arguments attempt to show, in other words, that a conjunction consisting of certain justified beliefs about the world and the proposition that, for example, the God of classical theism exists is a *contradiction* and thus cannot possibly be true.

Secondly, one has *evidential* arguments from evil, where the claim is instead that while the justified beliefs in question are logically compatible with the existence of the type of deity being considered, those justified beliefs provide *evidence against* the existence of such a deity. This evidence, moreover, is sufficiently strong to make it *more likely than not* that such a deity does not exist, thereby rendering belief in the existence of such a deity *irrational* in the absence of sufficiently strong countervailing considerations supporting the existence of such a deity.

The Structure of the Element

Section 1 addresses some preliminary issues that it is crucial to think about in formulating arguments from evil.

Section 2 is concerned with the question of how incompatibility arguments from evil are best formulated, with possible responses to incompatibility arguments. The specific argument offered there has two parts; the first aims at showing that no theodicy, or defense, or any combination, provides an answer to the argument, while the second part introduces additional premises needed to derive the conclusion that God does not exist.

Next, Section 3 focuses on skeptical theism – a theistic view that attempts to refute incompatibility arguments from evil by appealing to possible goods of *types* of which humans have no knowledge. A central conclusion will be that, given the argument developed in Section 2, skeptical theists have *much* more work to do to defend their claim of having defeated incompatibility versions of the argument from evil.

In Section 4, the discussion turns to evidential arguments from evil. There I set out the main alternatives, argue that some are unpromising, formulate an improved version of inference to the best explanation approaches, and conclude by slightly fine-tuning and defending what is arguably the most fundamental type of evidential argument from evil – namely, one based upon equiprobability principles.

1 Formulations of Arguments from Evil: Important Preliminary Issues

In the next section, I shall turn to the task of formulating a strong incompatibility argument from evil. Before doing that, however, some fundamental distinctions need to be considered: first, within normative or evaluative terms there is the distinction between axiological terms and deontological terms, which leads to the question of which should be used in formulating arguments from evil; secondly, there is the distinction between arguments from evil that involve only highly general claims about the evil found in the world, and those that involve much more specific claims; thirdly, there is the distinction between arguments that appeal only to readily observable facts about the world, and arguments involving premises that, though not matters of everyday observation, are claims for which very strong support can be offered.

1.1 Axiological Terms versus Deontological Terms: Which Should Be Used?

Evaluative or normative judgments are of various types. Some concern the moral status of actions, wherein one judges some actions to be morally wrong, others to be morally obligatory, and still others to be neither wrong nor obligatory, but simply morally permissible. Concepts involved in such judgments about what one ought or ought not do, one's duties, and the rights of individuals I shall refer to as *deontological* concepts.

We also make evaluative judgments, however, that, rather than involving claims about the moral status of actions, are judgments about the goodness or badness, the desirability or undesirability, of states of affairs. Most people, for example, think that pain is *intrinsically bad* – that is, that considered simply in itself, and ignoring consequences, being in pain is an undesirable state of affairs. Similarly, most people think that pleasurable experiences are *intrinsically good* – that is, that such experiences, taken simply in themselves, and without considering any consequences to which they may lead, are desirable. I shall refer to these concepts of goodness and badness, understood as desirability and undesirability, as *axiological* concepts.

Which concepts should be used in formulating arguments from evil, axiological or deontological? If the former, one might argue that since the world contains many intrinsically undesirable states of affairs, an omnipotent being could improve the world by eliminating such states of affairs. Thus one might argue – having in mind Leibniz's (1714) attempt in his *Monadology* (Paragraphs 53–55) to prove that this is the best of all possible worlds – that given the evil that exists, this is not the best of all possible worlds.

Any such approach seems unsatisfactory, however, since for any possible world, no matter how good, it would seem that a better world is possible. For let U be absolutely any world. Could there not be another world, W, consisting of U plus U*, where U* is an exact, qualitative duplicate of U? Then, however, if U were a good world, would not W be an even better world? If so, there cannot be a *best* of all possible worlds, since there would exist a never-ending sequence of better and better possible worlds. Consequently, the mere fact that an *omnipotent* being had failed to create the best of all possible worlds would not entail that such a being was less than perfectly good.

What, then, would be grounds for judging that an omnipotent being was less than morally perfect? The answer, it would seem, would be the existence of some evil that the omnipotent being could and *should* have prevented, but failed to do so. But then, should not incompatibility arguments from evil – and indeed, any arguments from evil – be formulated using *deontological* rather than axiological terms?

1.2 Highly General Propositions about Evils versus Much More Specific Propositions

Traditional formulations of incompatibility arguments from evil often involved only extremely general claims about evils found in the world. Sometimes, for example, they were based on the most general claim of all, namely, that the world contains at least one evil, at least one state of affairs whose existence should have been prevented if at all possible. At other times, reference was made to the existence of multiple, unspecified evils, or to the total amount of evil of which we are aware, or to the existence of individual but unspecified evils that are horrendous in nature.

Such formulations are silent on the *intrinsic nature* of the evils in question, thereby in effect assuming that such information is irrelevant to the incompatibility claim. Given certain responses to incompatibility arguments from evil, however, that view seems problematic. Consider, for example, free will responses, which claim that libertarian free will, where this involves the ability to perform actions not causally determined by states of affairs lying outside the agent's control, is very valuable, and that this value is such that it is better for persons to possess free will, even given that actions may be performed that will harm others and that are morally wrong. An omnipotent being could prevent such morally wrong actions, but the contention is that this would deprive people of the power to choose freely how to act and thus of something very valuable indeed.

There is much to be said about this 'free will defense' response to arguments from evil. My point here, however, is that rather than grappling with the difficult idea of libertarian free will, a defender of an incompatibility argument can try to render this type of defense *irrelevant*. They could do this, for example, by drawing a distinction between moral evils and natural evils – between evils resulting from immoral choices by free agents, and evils not so caused – and then by formulating an argument from evil in terms of natural evils.

Or consider another important response, namely, the 'soul-making' theodicy championed especially by John Hick, and which he traced back to a second century AD theologian, Irenaeus. This 'soul-making' theodicy involves the contention that the evils found in the world can be seen to be justified given the idea that God so designed the world to maximize the opportunity for people, through the exercise of free will in response to challenges that confront them, to grow spiritually in a way that would ultimately make them fit for communion with God:

> The value-judgement that is implicitly being invoked here is that one who has attained to goodness by meeting and eventually mastering temptations, and thus by rightly making responsible choices in concrete situations, is good in a richer and more valuable sense than would be one created *ab initio* in a state either of innocence or of virtue. In the former case, which is that of the actual moral achievements of mankind, the individual's goodness has within it the strength of temptations overcome, a stability based upon an accumulation of right choices, and a positive and responsible character that comes from the investment of costly personal effort. I suggest, then, that it is an ethically reasonable judgement, even though in the nature of the case not one that is capable of demonstrative proof, that human goodness slowly built up through personal histories of moral effort has a value in the eyes of the Creator which justifies even the long travail of the soul-making process. (1978, 255–6)

Hick's basic contentions, accordingly, are as follows. First, soul-making is a great good. Secondly, and as a result, God is justified in designing a world with that purpose in mind. Thirdly, our world is well designed in that regard. Consequently, if one views evil in the world as a problem, it is because, over-looking the great value of soul-making, one mistakenly thinks that the world ought, instead, to be a hedonistic paradise.

As with the free will defense, there are many strong objections to Hick's soul-making theodicy, but my point is once again that defenders of incompatibility arguments from evil can attempt to short-circuit all of that discussion by formulating things in terms of evils that are completely unnecessary for a soul-making world, by focusing, for example, upon the suffering of nonhuman animals over the eons before *Homo sapiens* arrived on the scene – suffering that makes no contribution to the development of anyone's moral character.

The moral, in short, is that there are reasons for thinking that, at least in the case of incompatibility arguments, stronger arguments can be formulated by focusing on *specific types* of evils, and it is striking how long it took philosophers to realize that this is so.

The breakthrough in this respect was due to William Rowe, who focused, first of all, in his 1979 article, "The Problem of Evil and Some Varieties of Atheism," upon the case of a fawn suffering a prolonged and agonizing death in a forest fire, and then, in his 1988 article, "Evil and Theodicy," upon the case of a five-year-old girl in Flint, Michigan, who was brutally beaten, raped, and then strangled by her mother's boyfriend. This shift, I believe, was important indeed.

1.3 Justified Beliefs versus What Is Known in Some Strong Sense of 'Knowledge'

Arguments from evil claim that there are propositions expressing facts about evils found in the world that are either incompatible with the existence of various deities – including the omnipotent, omniscient, and morally perfectly good deity of classical theism – or render the existence of the deity in question at least unlikely – and, arguably, extremely so. But what sorts of propositions can be employed in such arguments?

Suppose, for example, that a philosopher or theologian were to advance one of the following claims: (a) The suffering of nonhuman animals poses no problem, since nonhuman animals do not experience pain: all that one has is so-called 'pain behavior'; (b) there are no natural evils, only moral evils, since natural disasters such as the Lisbon earthquake, the eruption of Mount Vesuvius, the 1931 China floods, the 2004 Indian Ocean earthquake and tsunami, and so on are all caused by fallen angels, while the sufferings of animals due to predators such as tigers occur because predators are animals possessed by demons; (c) while humans and other animals suffer pain, that suffering is not undeserved, because the doctrines of reincarnation and karma are true. If the person then claims that the proposition in question is "true for all we *know*," what is one to say?

One may be tempted to reply that one *does* know that the proposition in question is false. Given, however, that there is no generally accepted analysis of the concept of knowledge nor even any close approximation thereto, replying in that way is surely to choose a path that is unlikely to be profitable. What one should say instead is, first, that the fundamental question here is what it is *reasonable* to believe, and secondly, that what it is reasonable to believe is not confined to propositions that are *known* in any sense of the latter term.

The moral is this. First, in formulating an incompatibility argument from evil, *any* propositions can be used that one is *justified in believing*. Secondly, if one is also justified in believing *the conjunction* of those propositions, and if that conjunction logically entails the nonexistence of the relevant deity, the result is a successful incompatibility argument from evil.

2 Incompatibility Arguments from Evil

In this section, I shall formulate a number of propositions that, taken together, are logically incompatible with the existence of God. Before doing that, however, I think it will be helpful to provide some background to readers new to this area by describing important responses to incompatibility arguments from evil.

First, one can offer a *theodicy*. This claims that while the world contains intrinsically evil states of affairs that may initially appear to be unjustified in the sense of not being logically necessary either for some good that outweighs the evil in question, or to avoid some greater evil, this initial impression is mistaken, since upon reflecting more deeply on the situation, it can be seen that there are known types of goods that justify the evils in question.

What are the alternatives to a theodicy? One involves arguing that for any evil that exists, it is *logically possible* that the evil is necessary either to avoid some still greater evil, or else to achieve some good outweighing the evil in question. Traditionally, such an alternative response was described as a *defense,* and it took the form of appealing to some *specific type* of good and saying that, for any evil that might appear unjustified, a good of that type could be present for all one knows, and that if it were, a deity would be justified in allowing the evil in question.

As an illustration, consider what is probably the most famous type of defense – namely, the free will defense – whose best-known defender is Alvin Plantinga (1974a, 7–64, and 1974b, 164–95). Here the basic ideas are that evils can be divided into moral evils and natural evils, and that allowing moral evils is justifiable because of the great good of there being agents who possess libertarian free will. As regards what are *described* as natural evils, such as the Lisbon earthquake, it is possible, for all we know, that those evils are in fact moral evils caused by the actions of nonhuman persons, including supernatural ones (1974a, 57–9, and 1974b, 191–3).

The crucial point about this way of arguing that certain evils in the world are logically compatible with the existence of God is that it does not appeal to the mere possibility of there being some *unknown* type of good that outweighs a given type of evil, and for which the evil is logically necessary, or to the mere possibility of there being some *unknown* type of evil that is weightier than the known evil, and that can only be avoided by allowing the known evil in question. Rather, a response such as Plantinga's specifies, first of all, a *type* of good – such as the existence and actions of genuinely free agents – possible instances of which might be prevented by God if God were to prevent what are generally described as 'natural evils.' It also specifies *how* the possible good in question is *connected* with the evil that it outweighs – namely, the free action in question is the cause of the evil.

More recently, however, many philosophers have championed a different way of arguing that the existence of all the evils found in the world is logically compatible with the existence of God. This approach is known as 'skeptical theism.' According to this view, there may be goods of which we have no knowledge – 'goods beyond our ken' – which, if they exist, justify God in allowing the evils present in the world. In contrast to traditional defenses, however, *nothing* is said here even about the *types* of goods in question, let alone about *how they are connected* to relevant, known evils.

The upshot is that the description typically offered of the idea of a defense – namely, as any attempt to show that the evils found in the world are logically compatible with the existence of God – is no longer satisfactory since it fails to distinguish between defenses and skeptical theism. Accordingly, I shall use the term 'defense' to refer to views that not only attempt to show that the evils found in the world are logically compatible with the existence of God, but also specify both *the type of goods* that are relevant and *how those goods are connected to the evils in question.*

Let me now describe the goal of this section in more detail. First of all, it is not to survey alternative incompatibility arguments from evil that have been advanced, nor is it to consider all of the various responses to such arguments and everything that can be said for and against such responses. As regards the former, many incompatibility arguments are weak, and my goal is to formulate what I hope is a stronger type of incompatibility argument. As regards the latter, while I shall sometimes comment, generally very briefly, on important responses, my object is to show that familiar theodicies and defenses are often rendered irrelevant by the incompatibility argument I shall set out.

Secondly, I shall not consider theodicies or defenses that appeal to supposedly *revealed* religious truths. A discussion of such approaches would require, in the end, arguing that there are good reasons to believe that the religions in question are false – a task that would require another and much longer book in itself.

Finally, as regards possible skeptical theist responses to the incompatibility argument I shall set out, that topic will be considered in Section 3.

2.1 The Existence of Suffering by Nonhuman Animals That Are Not Persons

Let me now develop the incompatibility argument in question and respond to objections.

(1) The world contains sentient nonpersons that undergo suffering, often intense, when they are killed by predators, by natural disasters such as forest fires, or by disease.

Objection to Proposition (1): Nonhuman animals do not experience pain.

Michael Murray, in the chapter entitled "Neo-Cartesianism" in his book *Nature Red in Tooth and Claw: Theism and the Problem of Animal Suffering*, appeals to a theory of consciousness typically advanced by philosophers who hold that all mental states are reducible to states involving nothing beyond the entities, properties, and relations postulated in theories in physics, and who maintain that for something to be a state of consciousness, it must be the object of a higher-order mental state – specifically, it must be the object of a higher-order *thought*. Such higher-order thought theories of consciousness – HOT theories for short – can, Murray points out, also be embraced by philosophers who are not physicalists with regard to the nature of mind and who hold that experiences involve phenomenal, 'raw feel' qualities – such as colors, sounds, tastes, and smells – that are not reducible to the stuff of physics. Given a HOT theory of consciousness, one can, accordingly, formulate a neo-Cartesian view of nonhuman animals, according to which they can be in states with phenomenal, nonphysical properties, but, since they lack the capacity for thought, they cannot have any higher-order thoughts and therefore are not conscious (2008, 55). The result, if one embraces this neo-Cartesian view, is that one can, according to Murray, plausibly hold that "so long as the animal lacks the higher-order access, so long as it cannot represent itself as being in a state of pain, there is nothing about its situation that has intrinsic moral disvalue" (2008, 56).

Murray's view is open to both philosophical and scientific objections. As regards the former, higher-order thought analyses of the concept of consciousness are open to decisive objections. It can be shown, for example, that if thoughts are themselves conscious states, the result is a vicious infinite regress, whereas if thoughts are not conscious states, then there can be purely mechanical devices that possess consciousness. Other serious philosophical objections have also been advanced against such analyses. Peter Carruthers, for example, arrived at the conclusion that it "may be that only humans, or perhaps humans and other species of great ape, are phenomenally conscious, if either of these forms of higher-order thought approach are correct" (2018, 192).

Then, as regards scientific objections, careful studies have found strong evidence that vertebrates can be in the same state as humans experiencing pain. First of all, the types of neural circuits present in the brains of humans when they experience pain are present in other mammals and in vertebrates as well. Secondly, opioid receptors are central in controlling pain (Kieffer 2007, 1), and such nonhuman animals also have opioid receptors. Thirdly, when given local anesthetics or analgesics, such nonhuman animals show reduced responses to noxious stimuli. Such scientific findings render implausible in the extreme any view that nonhuman animals do not have pain experiences similar to those of humans.

2.2 The Suffering by Nonhuman Animals Is Undeserved Suffering

(2) Suffering is deserved, at most, only if, acting as a free moral agent, one has done something morally wrong.

(3) Sentient nonpersons are not moral agents.

Therefore, from (2) and (3):

(4) All the suffering that sentient nonpersons undergo is undeserved suffering.
Objection to Proposition (4): The doctrines of karma and reincarnation show that this conclusion is false.

According to the idea of reincarnation, biological death is not the end of a person's existence, since a person will be reincarnated here on Earth in a different body. According to the doctrine of karma, however, a person either flourishes or suffers because of actions that person performed, either in the present life or in an earlier incarnation. So if a person suffers, that suffering is not undeserved: the suffering is punishment for earlier morally wrong behavior.

What about the suffering of nonhuman animals? This is explained in the same way, since if a human being behaves badly, the individual may be reincarnated not as a human, but as a nonhuman animal. So the suffering of nonhuman animals is also suffering they deserve to undergo because of misdeeds by the persons who are being reincarnated as nonhuman animals.

Several objections have been directed against theodicies based on this idea, including some by Whitley Kaufman (2005) in "Karma, Rebirth, and the Problem of Evil," which has generated substantial discussion. The crucial objections, however, seem to me to be the following. The first, directed against the doctrine of karma, is that nonhuman animals are not persons and therefore cannot be *identical* with moral agents who previously existed. Consequently, they cannot be justly punished for any immoral actions performed by previously existing persons.

The second objection is directed against the doctrine of reincarnation, and it is that humans do not have immaterial minds or souls. Consequently, reincarnation is ruled out.

Many people believe, however, that the question of whether humans have immaterial minds or souls is one that science cannot answer. But why do people think that this is so? The main reason, I suggest, is that the belief that humans have immaterial minds or souls is part of many religious worldviews in both the East and the West, and many people think that religious beliefs are not open to scientific investigation.

Is it plausible that the question of whether humans have immaterial minds or souls is not open to scientific investigation? After all, if humans have an immaterial mind or soul, that entity must surely stand in causal relations to the brain, and it would be surprising if everything at the physical level would then be just as it would be if no such entity existed. But if things at the physical level would be different if there were such an entity, scientific investigation can determine whether what one observes fits best with the view that humans have immaterial minds or souls, or with a denial of that view.

Before considering what happens when this is done, however, it is important to understand the main alternatives concerning the nature of the mind. There are three, commonly referred to as substance dualism, materialism/physicalism, and property dualism. According to substance dualism, the mind is an immaterial substance – that is, an entity capable of existing on its own, independently of any other thing, such as a body – and one that contains the ontological basis of all of one's psychological capacities and mental states. According to materialism/physicalism, in contrast, the mind is identical with the brain and involves nothing more than the fundamental particles, fields, and forces discovered by physics. Finally, according to property dualism – which is an intermediate view – while the categorical bases of all psychological *capacities* lie in the brain, sensory and other *experiences* involve *qualitative properties*, such as the color redness, the sound of a trumpet, the taste of salt, or the smell of lilacs, that are not reducible to the stuff of physics.

For reincarnation to be possible, substance dualism must be true, so let us consider what the outcome is when one investigates scientifically whether substance dualism is true. Here are some relevant facts – some requiring close scientific investigation, but others that are just a matter of everyday observation. First of all, a person who suffers a serious, but not fatal blow to the head may wind up unconscious. If the mind is the brain, the fact that a blow to the head, by affecting the brain, might cause loss of consciousness is not surprising. But why would this happen if the mind were an immaterial thing, capable of existing independently of the body? A blow to the head might well disrupt communications between the immaterial mind and parts of the brain, with the result that the individual's *external behavior* would be what we refer to as that of an 'unconscious' person, but there is no reason why the immaterial mind should cease having thoughts and feelings during that period of time.

Secondly, strokes, gunshot wounds, and so on can cause permanent damage to different parts of the brain, and it has been found not only that such injuries can affect both mental capacities and personality, but that precisely which psychological capacities or traits are impaired depends upon which part of the brain is damaged. Thus, damage to one part of the brain can affect ability to use language, while damage to another part can affect ability to think spatially; damage to yet another part can impair mathematical ability, while damage to another part can even alter personality.

Consider, for example, the part of the brain known as the occipital association cortex. It is divided into different regions, and here are some of the ways in which a person's psychological capacities can be affected by damage to certain regions:

> Some patients with lesions in area 19 on the left side lose their ability to read without losing their ability to write. Sometimes these patients can read individual letters and spell whole words without understanding them. Lesions in area 19 to fibers leading to the temporal lobe can result in a patient who can describe the features of an object without being able to say what the object is. Patients with lesions in area 37 can see faces without recognizing them, although they can describe the nose, cheeks, mouth, etc. These same patients can identify objects by class, but not by specific type. For example, the patient can say whether an object is a car, a bird or a tree, but cannot say whether it is a Volkswagen, an eagle or a pine. (Best 2018, Ch. 6)

None of this is surprising if the mind *is* the brain, for then the bases for psychological capacities, personality traits, memories, and so on are complex neuronal circuits. In contrast, if the mind were an immaterial entity, these results would be utterly unexpected and would have to be given completely *ad hoc* explanations.

Thirdly, certain diseases radically affect mental function, memories, and so on. Alzheimer's disease is among the most familiar, with effects so extreme over time that it is quite natural to think that the person who once existed no longer does. But how could a disease ever have such an effect upon an immaterial mind? If memories are states of an immaterial substance, why are they destroyed, or why is it that the immaterial mind is unable to access those states? If, however, memories are instead stored in various parts of the brain, with working memory located in parts of the frontal lobe, long-term memory for events in the parietal lobe, and long-term memories of life events in the temporal lobe, and if recalling a memory requires activation in the frontal lobe (Best 2018, Ch. 8), there is nothing surprising about a disease such as Alzheimer's.

Fourthly, there is aging, where not only the body but also the mind typically deteriorates, so that various psychological capacities, such as memory, gradually decline. Once again, if the mind is the brain, there is nothing surprising here: the brain is deteriorating with age, along with the rest of the body. In contrast, there is no reason why an immaterial mind should deteriorate with age, so the decline of the mind as one grows older is a puzzle, and not at all what one would expect on the hypothesis that the mind is an immaterial substance.

Fifthly, and as is both obvious to everyday observation, and as has been shown by numerous psychological experiments, the mental capacities of very young members of our species gradually increase as they mature. Again, there is nothing surprising in this if the mind is the brain: neuronal circuits that are the physical bases of the capacities in questions gradually get built up over time. But why would there be such changes if the mind were an immaterial substance?

Sixthly, there is the phenomenon of inheritance, in which the probability that a given individual will have certain psychological traits or abilities is a function of the presence or absence of those traits in his or her parents. If the mind is an immaterial substance, what explains this fact? Why should there be any correlation between the personality traits and abilities present in the immaterial minds of a person's parents and those present in the person's own immaterial mind?

Seventhly, there are greater psychological similarities between identical twins than between fraternal twins. For example, the correlation with regard to IQ between identical twins reared together has been shown in many studies to be around 0.85, whereas, for fraternal twins reared together, the correlation is around 0.55. If the mental abilities that enter into IQ have their basis in structures in the brain, then we would expect a significantly greater correlation for identical twins than for fraternal twins. But if intellectual abilities reside instead in an immaterial mind, what possible explanation could there be for such a difference in correlations in IQ between identical twins on the one hand and fraternal twins on the other?

Eighthly, psychotropic drugs can affect mood greatly, relieve depression and anxiety, give rise to paranoia or reduce it, and so on. Once again, if the mind is the brain, and emotional states depend upon chemicals in the brain, this all falls into place. In contrast, these things are not at all what we would expect if the mind were an immaterial substance. For why should Valium or Prozac affect an immaterial substance?

Finally, the mental differences both between humans and other animals and between different species of nonhuman animals correlate with differences in the structures present in the relevant brains. If psychological capacities have their bases in neuronal structures, this is once again precisely what one would expect and predict. But what is the explanation if the mind is an immaterial substance? Why, for example, do humans have a more highly developed brain if their superior psychological capacities belong not to the brain but to an immaterial mind?

In short, many phenomena – some very familiar, others much less so – would be not only surprising and mysterious but also hard to explain if the mind were an immaterial substance. By contrast, however, those phenomena are perfectly explainable if the mind is, instead, the brain. The conclusion, accordingly, is that there is massive evidence against the view that the mind is an immaterial substance.

It is not surprising, then, that in the science concerned with the nature of the mind – namely, psychology – one has to search long and hard to find researchers who believe that the mind is an immaterial substance.

We arrive, accordingly, at the following conclusion:

(5) Humans do not have immaterial minds or souls.

Consequently, one cannot refute proposition (4) by appealing to the doctrines of karma and reincarnation.

2.3 A Physicalist Alternative to Reincarnation?

Reincarnation, by definition, involves a soul's being reborn in a new body. Some philosophers have argued, however, that humans can survive death even if they do not have immaterial minds or souls, and by a number of routes. One way, for example, proposed by Peter van Inwagen (1978, 120–1), is that shortly after death, before the body has undergone decay, God replaces the corpse of a person who has just died with a simulacrum (1978, 120–1).

Most of these proposals, however, are open to serious objections. Some of these are succinctly and forcefully set out by Hud Hudson (2001, 180–7). Hudson goes on, however, to offer his own account, which perhaps, given some minor tweaking, is a plausible defense of the view that it is *logically possible* that humans, even if they are purely material beings, could survive death (2001, 187–92).

Does this make it possible to resurrect the karma response to arguments from evil? The answer is that it does not, since the bodies of currently living sentient nonpersons do not stand in the types of causal relations needed for them to be identical with things that lived earlier. This, together with (5), gives us:

(6) Neither current humans nor sentient nonpersons are identical with living things that lived and died earlier.

2.4 A Soul-Making Theodicy Is Also Ruled Out

Since most nonhuman animals are not persons, John Hick's "soul-making" theodicy would also initially seem to be rendered irrelevant. Trent

Dougherty, however, argues that some nonhuman animals "will become full-fledged persons (rational substances) who can look back on their lives – both pre- and post-personal – and form attitudes about what has happened to them and how they fit into God's plan" (2014, 3). If so, a soul-making theodicy could be invoked for the suffering endured by sentient nonpersons.

For this to provide a counter to any argument from evil, it must be *reasonable* to believe either that sentient nonpersons have immaterial souls or that they are somehow resurrected. The former claim, however, is no more reasonable as regards sentient nonpersons than as regards persons, nor, in the absence of good reasons for accepting some particular religious revelation, is it reasonable to believe that either humans or other animals continue to live after their biological deaths on earth. Thus we have:

(7) The suffering of sentient nonpersons cannot be justified by a soul-making theodicy.

2.5 The Suffering in Question Is Not Caused by Moral Agents

(8) We have extremely well-confirmed scientific accounts of the evolutionary origin of predatory animals and of their behavior, and, similarly, of the causes of natural disasters and of the existence of disease-causing organisms, such as bacteria and viruses, and those accounts do not involve any references to activity on the part of moral agents, supernatural or otherwise.

Therefore it is very reasonable to believe that

(9) Neither the existence nor the activities of predatory animals are caused by any moral agents, and the same is true for natural disasters and diseases.

Therefore, from (1) and (9):

(10) The suffering in question that is endured by sentient nonpersons results from natural causes, and is not caused by moral agents.

Therefore, from (10):

(11) Preventing the undeserved suffering that sentient nonpersons undergo when they are killed by predators, natural disasters, or diseases would not interfere with the free actions of any moral agents.

Some Comments on the Argument to this Point

1. Proposition (11) renders irrelevant important types of theodicies and defenses – namely, those appealing to the concept of, and the claimed value of libertarian free will. The same is true, moreover, for a crucial part of the theodicy advanced by Richard Swinburne, who contends that a person needs to have the power to cause great harm. The idea is that if the actions open to an individual vary enormously in moral worth, libertarian free will is very valuable indeed. On the other hand, if the variation in the moral status of what one can do is limited, then libertarian free will adds much less to the world: one has what has been characterized as a 'toy world,' where one has very little responsibility for the well-being of others:

> [I]f my responsibility for you is limited to whether or not to give you some quite unexpected new piece of photographic equipment, but I cannot make you unhappy, or stunt your growth, or limit your education, then I do not have a great deal of responsibility for you. If God gave agents only such limited responsibility for their fellows, He would not have given much. He would be like a father asking his elder son to look after the younger son, and adding that he would be watching the elder son's every move and would intervene the moment the elder son did anything wrong. The elder son might justly retort that while he would be happy to share his father's work, he could only really do so if he was left to make his own judgments as to what to do within a significant range of the options available to the father. (1996, 39)

2. There are various objections to any appeal to libertarian free will, with perhaps the most important being that there is no agreement among philosophers that any satisfactory analysis of this concept has ever been advanced. In addition, given the conclusion that humans do not have immaterial minds, any appeal to the idea of libertarian free will needs to show that any analysis offered – involving, for example, the idea of agent causation – is compatible with the mind's being a material substance.

The following theodicies and defenses, in any case, have been eliminated by the simple strategy of focusing on the pain endured by sentient nonpersons: soul-making theodicies, karma plus reincarnation/resurrection theodicies, and all free will theodicies and defenses, including Swinburne's 'freedom to cause great harm' theodicy. What important theodicies and defenses still need to be addressed?

One of the more common responses to arguments from evil appeals to the idea that the undeserved suffering that individuals endure will be more than compensated by the quality of the life they experience after death. Given the extremely strong evidence that the human mind is identical with the brain, however, the only possible way in which conscious beings might survive death would be if there was a bodily resurrection. This, however, is a religious belief, and, as indicated earlier, it is not possible here to consider religious theodicies or defenses.

Are there, then, any further important theodicies or defenses, not based upon religious claims, that need to be addressed? The answer is that there is one, to which I shall now turn.

2.6 Allowing Undeserved Suffering Cannot Be Justified by Appealing to the Great Good of the Existence of Laws of Nature

An appeal to laws of nature is often introduced to deal with the problem of natural evils – as is done, for example, by Richard Swinburne (1998, 182–198) – and this type of approach involves the following claims: first, it is important that events exhibit regular patterns, since otherwise people would not know what effects their actions might have; secondly, this will not be so unless events are governed by natural laws; thirdly, if events are governed by natural laws, the operation of those laws will give rise to occurrences that harm individuals; and thus, fourthly, God's creating a world containing natural evils is justified because the existence of natural evils is entailed by natural laws, and a world without natural laws would be a much worse world.

Such theodicies are open to serious objections. First, it is generally held that an omnipotent deity could miraculously intervene at any time and place to alter what happens in the natural world, and this is surely right, since if God is the creator of everything, all that is needed for God to be able to intervene in the natural world at any time is to create laws that, rather than being of the form

"Whenever a natural event of type F happens, it will causally give rise to an event of type G"

are instead of the form

"Whenever a natural event of type F happens, *and God does not will that it not be followed by an event of type G*, the event of type F will causally give rise to an event of type G."

Laws could, in short, be of the 'God willing' variety. Moreover, they need to be of that variety if, as most theists believe, God sometimes intervenes miraculously in the natural world.

Given such laws, God, by occasionally intervening in a miraculous fashion, could prevent great evils. Even if those interventions were so dramatic that humans would necessarily view them as cases of divine intervention, this would not render effective human action impossible, since the rarity of such occurrences would not undermine the belief that events almost always occur in accordance with natural laws.

In response, it can be argued that any such dramatic intervention to prevent evils that would otherwise result due to natural causes would in fact be undesirable, since it is morally very important that God remain hidden, which would not be the case if God intervened in such a way to prevent natural evils.

The question of whether, if God exists, it is desirable that he generally remains hidden, is an important one. But it is not necessary to address that question here, since, as we shall now see, there are very strong objections to the 'laws of nature' theodicy that are completely independent of the question of whether it is, or is not, desirable for God to remain generally hidden.

Let us turn, then, to a second argument, which is that many evils depend upon precisely *what* laws the world contains. An omnipotent being could, for example, easily create a world with the same laws of *physics* as our world, but with slightly different laws linking neurophysiological states to qualities of experiences, so that extremely intense pains either never occur, or else could be turned off by the sufferer when they served no purpose. Alternatively, God could create additional physical laws of a rather specialized sort that could, for example, either cause very harmful viruses to self-destruct, or prevent viruses such as the avian flu virus from evolving into an airborne form that would have the capacity to kill hundreds of million people.

Some philosophers, most notably Peter van Inwagen, have questioned whether God could have created a world where the laws differed in any significant way from the laws of the actual world. Thus van Inwagen, discussing the designing of worlds in his book *The Problem of Evil*, says,

> Our own universe provides the only model we have for the formidable task of designing a world. (For all we know, in every possible world that exhibits any degree of complexity, the laws of nature are the actual laws. There are, in fact, philosophically minded physicists who believe that there is only one possible set of laws of nature, and it is epistemically possible that they are right.) (2006, 117)

A thorough discussion of this would take us far afield, into both philosophy of mind and the epistemology and metaphysics of modality – that is, of logical possibility and logical necessity. As regards philosophy of mind, many present-day philosophers believe that all entities, all properties, and all relations are reducible to the entities, properties, and relations postulated by theories in physics. Many other philosophers, however, as noted earlier, believe that, on the contrary, the sensory qualities present in experience – colors, sounds, smells, tastes, and so on – while *caused* by complex neural states, are *not themselves reducible* to the entities, properties, and relations in physics. If this is right, then *physics* can never provide a total theory of everything, since what exists will include the nonphysical properties present in sensory experiences, together with, at least, causal laws linking complex neural states to conscious experiences involving those properties – laws that by definition will not be laws of physics.

Physics itself, moreover, cannot provide any reason for thinking either that this property dualist view is right, or that it is not, so physicists who express any opinions on this matter are speaking not as physicists but as amateur philosophers. Consequently, van Inwagen's appeal to physics provides no ground at all for holding that there could not be *psychological* laws enabling individuals to turn off painful experiences when they wanted to do so.

What about the possibility that the laws of physics themselves might be different? Unless one holds that the idea of laws of the 'God willing' variety are logically impossible, the fundamental laws that govern physical events could either contain a theological condition or not do so. The claim that only one possibility exists for laws of nature is, accordingly, very implausible.

If this conclusion is right, it can be generalized. Suppose that some theory L contains all the laws of physics. What would be the logical form of a 'God willing' law corresponding to L? A natural answer would be as follows:

> If there is no proposition p about the state of the world at time t such that God wills that proposition p be true, then the state of the world at time t depends only on L together with how the world was at times earlier than t. However, if there is some proposition p about the state of the world at time t such that God wills that proposition p be true, then the state of the world at time t will be one where p is true but everything else is as close to the way things would have been if God had not willed that p be true.

A 'God willing' law, thus formulated, is the conjunction of two propositions. What reason could there be, then, for holding that the following proposition, of the same logical form, could not express a law of nature?

> If there are not going to be any viruses or bacteria at time t that will harm either humans or other sentient beings, then the state of the world at time t depends only on L together with how the world was at times earlier than t. However, if there are going to be any viruses or bacteria at time t that will harm humans or other sentient beings, then the state of the world at time t will be one where the fundamental particles that would have composed those viruses and bacteria at time t will be rearranged in a minimal way so that those viruses and bacteria do not exist at time t, while everything else will be as close to the way things would have been if there were not going to be any viruses or bacteria at time t that would harm humans or other sentient beings.

One final point needs to be made about laws of the sort just described. Van Inwagen, in his discussion (2006, 114), employs the following proposition in the story he offers as a defense against the argument from evil:

(3) Being massively irregular is a defect in a world, a defect at least as great as the defect of containing patterns of suffering mentally equivalent to those found in the actual world.

What is it for a world to be "massively irregular"? Van Inwagen's answer is this: "A *massively irregular world* is a world in which the laws of nature fail in some massive way" (2006, 114). But how many times must the laws of nature fail for the failure to be massive? As noted earlier, van Inwagen has suggested that human beings may survive death by God's miraculously replacing the corpse of a person who has just died with a simulacrum (1978, 120–1), and given that many estimates of the number of humans that have ever lived are around 100 billion, the number of failures of laws of nature needed before van Inwagen considers a world to be massively irregular is apparently very large indeed.

If there were a 'God willing' law, and if God frequently willed that certain propositions were true at various times, would van Inwagen claim that one had a massively irregular world? Perhaps he would, since he formulates the idea of a massively irregular world with reference specifically to the laws of *physics*. But then van Inwagen's proposition (3) would be extremely odd. Why should irregularity *with regard to the laws of physics* have great negative value if those 'laws' were *not* laws in the strict sense, as would be the case if all laws were 'God willing' laws? Should not the crucial fact then be that, as regards the real, underlying laws of nature – namely, the 'God willing' laws – there would be absolutely no irregularities at all?

Proposition (3) is also morally odd, since it assigns more weight to something that sounds like an aesthetic value – the absence of massive irregularity – than to the totality of all of the suffering the world contains – something of great moral significance indeed.

In addition, I have described an alternative to 'God willing' laws that involves only somewhat more complex, purely physical laws. There would then be no irregularities at all given laws of that kind, since van Inwagen's definition of "a massively irregular world" is one where the laws of nature "fail" in some massive way, and under the alternative in question to 'God willing' laws, there would never be any failure of any law.

To return to the main argument, given 'God willing' laws, God could intervene to destroy the viruses and bacteria that are responsible for diseases that cause enormous suffering and millions of deaths each year. These diseases include, in the case of viruses, AIDS, cervical cancer, dengue fever, Ebola

disease, hepatitis, influenza, Lassa fever, measles, Nipah virus disease, polio-
myelitis, rabies, rotavirus, viral hemorrhagic fever, and West Nile fever. In the
case of bacteria, they include anthrax, bacterial meningitis, bacterial pneumo-
nia, diphtheria, epidemic typhus, leprosy, leptospirosis, Lyme disease, menin-
gococcal meningitis, necrotizing fasciitis, pelvic inflammatory disease,
rheumatic fever, scarlet fever, tetanus, toxic shock syndrome, tuberculosis,
typhoid fever, and yaws. Alternatively, if God preferred, precisely the same
result could be achieved by God's creating purely physical laws that result in the
destruction of harmful viruses and bacteria as soon they come into being. There
would never have been, then, the Black Death in the Middle Ages, which is
estimated to have killed between 75 and 200 million people, or the 1918 flu
pandemic, which killed between 50 and 100 million people.

God could also intervene whenever it was necessary to prevent great natural
disasters in the form of earthquakes, floods, tidal waves, hurricanes, and so on.
These would include the earthquake in China in 1556 that killed around 800,000
people, or tsunamis, such as the one in 2004 that hit twelve Asian countries and
killed over 200,000 people.

Finally, it is not just natural evils that God could have prevented.
Consider great moral evils such as the Holocaust. A small intervention
by an omnipotent, omniscient, and perfectly good being could have
allowed one of the many failed attempts to assassinate Hitler to succeed,
or a small mental nudge could have resulted in Hitler's realizing the error
of his deadly anti-Semitism.

The irrelevance of an appeal to the claimed desirability of God's remaining
relatively hidden is also now apparent. Natural disasters like floods, hurricanes,
tornadoes, and droughts all depend upon the weather in ways that involve highly
complex causal processes. Would any human conclude that God must be
intervening if hurricanes never occurred in human history? Would it not require
an unimaginably massive scientific inquiry, if it were even possible, for humans
to arrive at the conclusion that some supernatural being must be intervening to
prevent such occurrences? Or consider earthquakes, which occur at the bound-
aries of tectonic plates. If God simply prevented such movement, or allowed it
to occur only very slowly, would any human ever be able to discover what was
happening?

The same is true with regard to the suffering and deaths that result from
diseases, including those listed above, due to viruses and bacteria. An omnipotent and omniscient being would know, as he watched things evolve, when any
new virus or bacterium that appeared would harm humans or other sentient
beings, and could destroy any such thing immediately. Or he could have created
laws that would do that without any intervention needed on his part. If either

were the case, would any human ever be able to discover that this was happening?

Finally, the same is true as regards great moral evils. An omniscient being would know when a Stalin or a Hitler or a Hirohito was about to do something that would lead to the deaths of millions. If such people died from a stroke, would anyone know that a deity had intervened?

The conclusion, in short, is that if there were an omnipotent and omniscient being, all of the suffering and deaths due to natural disasters and to viruses and diseases could have been prevented if such a being so chose, and the same is true of great moral evils. Moreover, no human person would ever know that this had been done unless that deity chose to communicate that fact to humans. An appeal to the claimed desirability of the hiddenness of God does nothing to block, accordingly, any well-formulated version of the argument from evil.

The upshot is that there is good reason to accept the following conclusion:

(12) Preventing the undeserved suffering that sentient nonpersons undergo when they are killed by predators, natural disasters, or diseases cannot be justified by an appeal either to the great value of there being laws of nature, or to the claimed desirability of a deity's remaining hidden.

2.7 Summing Up Part 1 of the Incompatibility Argument from Evil: No Nonreligious Theodicy or Defense Provides a Satisfactory Answer to the Present Incompatibility Argument from Evil

As we have seen, the argument, as developed to this point, renders soul-making theodicies irrelevant, as well as free will theodicies and defenses, including Swinburne's variant. Also, the contentions that sentient nonpersons do not experience pain, and that sentient nonpersons are identical to persons who existed previously, are open to extremely strong scientific objections. Finally, neither an appeal to the value of laws of nature, nor to the claimed desirability of God's remaining hidden, provides a satisfactory defense for the existence of natural evils.

Is any other nonreligious theodicy or defense a serious candidate for being a satisfactory response to the first part of the incompatibility argument from evil I have set out? I do not think that there is. If that is right, we have the following conclusion:

(13) No nonreligious theodicy or defense provides a satisfactory answer to the incompatibility argument from evil that has been set out.

2.8 Part 2 of the Incompatibility Argument from Evil

The argument does not yet, however, entail that God does not exist, since we have not yet considered the possibility of types of goods and evils of which we have no knowledge, and whose existence would justify the evils present in the world. For this possibility to obtain, however, the mere existence of goods beyond our ken whose greatness outweighed the evils found in the world would not be sufficient. In addition, the evils in question would have to be *logically necessary* for the existence of those unknown goods. I shall now argue, however, that the latter is not possible. If that is right, it will follow that God does exist.

Under What Conditions Is Allowing Undeserved Suffering Morally Permissible?

The starting point involves asking when not preventing undeserved suffering, when one could have done so, is morally permissible, and the answer proposed is as follows:

(14) Refraining from preventing some person or sentient nonperson from undergoing undeserved suffering when one could prevent that suffering at no cost to oneself is morally permissible, *at most*, when one of the following four conditions obtains:

Condition 1: Preventing the undeserved suffering would interfere with the free action of some moral agent.

Condition 2: Allowing the undeserved suffering would lead to an improvement in the life of the individual undergoing the suffering, an improvement that otherwise could not be achieved, and where the improvement would outweigh the badness of the undeserved suffering.

Condition 3: Preventing the undeserved suffering would result in some other sentient being undergoing even greater undeserved suffering.

Condition 4: Not preventing the undeserved suffering would make possible either the existence of some intrinsically good state of affairs, or the prevention of some intrinsically bad state of affairs, which would otherwise be impossible, and which would outweigh the *prima facie* wrongness of allowing the undeserved suffering of the sentient being.

Under What Conditions Is an Omnipotent and Omniscient *Being's Allowing Undeserved Suffering Morally Permissible?*

The next step in the argument involves determining when, in view of proposition (14), it would be morally permissible for an omnipotent and omniscient being to allow undeserved suffering, the goal being to show that this would never be morally permissible. The argument is as follows.

(15) An omnipotent and omniscient being can prevent any undeserved suffering at no cost to himself.

It then follows from (14) and (15) that

(16) An omnipotent and omniscient being can morally refrain from preventing any sentient being from undergoing undeserved suffering only if either condition 1, condition 2, condition 3, or condition 4 obtains.

Condition 1 Could Not Obtain for an Omnipotent and Omniscient Being

Recall the following proposition from Section 2.5:

(11) Preventing the undeserved suffering that sentient nonpersons undergo when they are killed by predators, natural disasters, or diseases does not interfere with the free actions of any moral agents.

It follows from (11) that

(17) As regards preventing the suffering that sentient nonpersons undergo due to predation, natural disasters, or diseases, condition 1 does not obtain for anyone, including an omnipotent and omniscient being.

Condition 2 Could Not Obtain for an Omnipotent and Omniscient Being

The argument concerning the nonsatisfaction of condition 2 is then:

(18) Any suffering that sentient nonpersons undergo when they are being killed by predators, natural disasters, or diseases does not improve the quality of life of the sentient nonperson that is being killed.

Therefore:

(19) Condition 2 does not obtain.

Condition 3 Could Not Obtain for an Omnipotent and Omniscient Being

Next, the argument for the nonsatisfaction of condition 3 is as follows:

(20) Preventing some sentient nonperson P from undergoing undeserved suffering can never *by itself logically entail* that some other sentient being Q undergoes undeserved suffering that one could have prevented had one not prevented P's undeserved suffering.

(21) For any propositions *p* and *q*, an omnipotent being can make it the case that *p* without making it the case that *q* unless *p* entails *q*.

Therefore, from (20) and (21):

(22) An omnipotent and omniscient being would be able to prevent all undeserved suffering by sentient nonpersons without that resulting in any undeserved suffering by any other sentient being.

Therefore, from (22):

(23) Condition 3 does not obtain.

Condition 4 Could Not Obtain for an Omnipotent and Omniscient Being

(24) The only intrinsically good or intrinsically bad states of affairs are ones involving properties of, or relations between, *conscious* beings, either persons or nonpersons.

(25) Allowing a sentient being P to experience undeserved suffering S could be a necessary condition of enabling some other sentient being Q to be in an intrinsically desirable state D, or to avoid being in an intrinsically undesirable state U, only if either P's being in state S is causally or nomologically necessary for Q's being in state D or not being in state U, or else Q's being in state D, or not being in state U, logically entails that P is in state S.

(26) As regards causal and nomological connections, an omnipotent being can bring it about that Q is in state D, or not in state U, without P's undergoing the undeserved suffering S, by creating either laws of the 'God willing' variety, or else more complex laws, either of physics or psychology, according to which P's being in state S is not causally or nomologically necessary for Q's being in state D, or not being in state U.

Therefore, from (25) and (26):

(27) An omnipotent and omniscient being can be justified in not preventing undeserved suffering S on the part of a sentient being P in order to bring it about that some other sentient being Q is in an intrinsically desirable state D,

or not in an intrinsically undesirable state U, at most, only if Q's being in state D, or not being in state U, logically entails P's being in a state S of undeserved suffering.

(28) The only way that a sentient being Q's being in state D, or not being in state U, can logically entail that some other sentient being P is in a state S of undeserved suffering is if being in D, or not being in U, is, or else involves, either of the following: (a) a true belief by Q that P is in a state S of undeserved suffering, or (b) the satisfaction of a desire by Q that P be in a state S of undeserved suffering.

(29) Believing truly that P is in a state S of undeserved suffering is no more valuable than believing truly that P is not in a state S of undeserved suffering, so an omnipotent being's preventing P from being in a state S of undeserved suffering does not entail that Q will be any worse off as regards the possession of true beliefs.

(30) There are some desires the satisfaction of which is not intrinsically good, among which is the desire that someone else endure undeserved suffering.

(31) It is not morally wrong to deprive a sentient being of the satisfaction of a desire that is not intrinsically good, such as the desire that someone endure undeserved suffering.

It follows from (27), (28), (29), (30), and (31) that

(32) There is no intrinsically good state D, or intrinsically bad state U, such that an omnipotent being's preventing a sentient being P from enduring undeserved suffering would logically entail that the omnipotent being had wrongly made some other sentient being Q worse off in virtue of the fact that that sentient being would not be in state D, or would be in state U.

It then follows from (25), (26), and (32) that

(33) Condition 4 does not obtain.

An Omnipotent and Omniscient Being Is Never Justified in Not Preventing Undeserved Suffering by a Sentient Nonperson

It follows from (14), (17), (19), (23), and (33) that

(34) An omnipotent and omniscient being is never justified in not preventing the undeserved suffering of sentient nonpersons.

Conclusion of the Incompatibility from Evil Argument:
The Nonexistence of God

(35) A being that does something that is not morally justified is not morally perfect.

It then follows from (1), (4), (34), and (35) that

(36) There is no omnipotent, omniscient, and morally perfect person.

(37) God is by definition omnipotent, omniscient, and morally perfect.

Therefore, from (36) and (37):

(38) God does not exist.

2.9 Some Comments on the Above Argument

In formulating this incompatibility argument from evil, a central goal was to block various responses to which incompatibility versions of the argument from evil are often exposed. Thus, first of all, the argument, rather than referring to a number of different types of evil – something that is perfectly reasonable in evidential formulations of the argument from evil – focuses specifically on suffering endured by sentient nonpersons. This was done to render irrelevant 'soul-making' theodicies. Similarly, free will theodicies and defenses were ruled out by incorporating the factual claim that neither animal predation nor natural disasters and diseases are caused by moral agents, a claim very strongly supported by our scientific knowledge of such events.

Secondly, although my own preferred approach to normative ethics is a deontological one, another goal in constructing the above argument was that it be compatible with a consequentialist approach to ethics. Thus, among the situations that might justify one in not preventing the occurrence of undeserved suffering, cases were included where not preventing the suffering would make it possible to achieve intrinsically good states of affairs that would outweigh the *prima facie* wrongness of allowing the undeserved suffering of persons or sentient nonpersons.

Finally, although the argument is compatible with a consequentialist approach to normative ethics, it is incompatible with an *unqualified* desire-satisfaction consequentialist approach, since one of the premises of the argument is that the satisfaction of a desire that another individual undergo undeserved suffering is *not* intrinsically good. I do not think, however, that that can be the basis of a serious objection to the argument, since I think that few ethicists would think that positive value should be assigned to the satisfaction of sadistic preferences.

3 Skeptical Theism: Human Epistemological Limitations and Incompatiblity Arguments from Evil

3.1 Skeptical Theism

Perhaps as a result of the failure, albeit not always acknowledged, of traditional theodicies and defenses, some philosophers have recently been pursuing a very different approach, known as *skeptical theism*. What is skeptical theism? As the name suggests, it is the combination of theism with some skeptical claim, so one needs only to specify the skeptical claim in question. The answer is, first of all, that it is "skepticism about the realm of potentially God-justifying reasons" (Bergmann 2009, 375). But secondly, it cannot be an *all-encompassing* skepticism about that realm, since a theist who holds that belief in God is justified must think that one is justified in believing that there are God-justifying reasons. So what is the skeptical claim? The answer is that it is the contention that facts about the natural world, including the goods and evils found therein, provide *no basis at all* for any justified beliefs about the *probability* of the existence or nonexistence of unknown goods that would serve as reasons that would justify God, if he existed, in allowing the evils that the world contains.

What is one to say about the skeptical component? Is it a neutral thesis that nontheists might well accept? Bergmann apparently thinks so: "although nontheists won't endorse skeptical theism given its *theistic* component, many think that nontheists should – and some do – endorse its *skeptical* component" (2009, 375). In fact, however, and first of all, no nontheist should accept that thesis, *except as part of a much more inclusive skeptical thesis*. To see why, notice that one way in which a person can be a nontheist is by being what might be called a demonist, where I am using that term to refer, not to someone who worships a supposedly fallen angel but, instead, to a person who believes – presumably unhappily – that there is an omnipotent, omniscient, *and perfectly evil* being. One can then imagine an 'ademonist' advancing an argument from goodness against the existence of such a being, along with a skeptical demonist who advocates skepticism about the realm of potentially Demon-justifying reasons for there being good states of affairs in the world. (Compare Morriston's "Skeptical Demonism.")

The crucial point, however, is that, as we shall see in Section 4, the skeptical theist's belief on this matter is *demonstrably* wrong. First of all, there is a principle that is absolutely fundamental to inductive inferences that enables one to prove, for example, that the probability that any *prima facie* evil is also an evil given the totality of goods and evils that exist, *both known and unknown*, is greater than one-half. Secondly, by considering multiple *prima facie* evils, one can show that the probability that there is a God-justifying reason for allowing the evils found in the world is very low indeed.

3.2 Arguments for Skeptical Theism's Skeptical Thesis

Let us consider, nevertheless, the support that has been offered for the skeptical thesis that is part of skeptical theism, and which can take quite different forms, as described in detail in Trent Dougherty's excellent article (2016) on this topic. Basically, the support offered is of three main kinds. First, there is the approach, defended, for example, by Stephen Wykstra (1984 and 1996), and Daniel Howard-Snyder (2009), that involves offering reasons for thinking that if God exists, there will be good-making properties that we humans are not aware of. Secondly, there is the type of theistic skepticism championed by Peter van Inwagen (1991 and 2006), which rests upon a very strong form of *modal* skepticism – that is, skepticism concerning our ability to arrive at justified beliefs about what things are possible – augmented by an equally strong form of *moral* skepticism. Finally, there is the type of argument advanced by Michael Bergman (2001 and 2009), which involves claims about when certain inductive arguments are justified.

Wykstra and Howard-Snyder appeal to a variety of considerations to support the version of skeptical theism that they advance. Wykstra, for example, appeals to a parent analogy, the idea being that just as in treating a child's illness it may be necessary to inflict pain on a child who cannot understand why we are doing that, so God may have to allow evils where we humans cannot grasp God's reasons for doing so. Howard-Snyder, on the other hand, argues, first, that there has been moral progress, during which it has only gradually been realized that certain things are intrinsically good and other things intrinsically evil, and that there is good reason to think that such moral progress is not yet at an end. Consequently, it is reasonable to believe that there may be kinds of intrinsic goods of which we have, as yet, no knowledge.

Wykstra's parent analogy has been criticized by a number of philosophers, including Bruce Russell (1988, 147ff.), William Rowe (1996, 274ff., 2001, 298, and 2006, 89), and Trent Dougherty (2011). All of them in effect offer a defense of the "reverse parent analogy," which Dougherty (2016, 14) describes as follows:

> Just as we would necessarily expect a loving parent with the power to do so to make a necessarily suffering child understand the reasons for her suffering, so we would expect a loving God who clearly has the power to do so to make us able to understand the reason for our suffering.

Dougherty claims – and plausibly, I think – that the reverse parent analogy is stronger than the parent analogy.

If this is right, it would seem that a parallel objection applies to Howard-Snyder's line of argument. For the world to contain very great suffering for which we can see no reason is unsatisfactory in the extreme, and it is reasonable to think that a loving God should enable us to have some idea, *however incomplete it may be*, both of what the relevant, counterbalancing goods are, and of why it is impossible for those goods to exist without the suffering.

Next, consider the second way of attempting to argue for skeptical theism – Peter van Inwagen's approach, which involves both modal skepticism and moral skepticism. The former was evident in his claim that it is epistemically possible that physicists who believe that there is only one logically possible set of laws may be right (2006, 117). In response to that claim, I argued that there are no grounds that one can offer for ruling out 'God willing' laws, and then that, if they are possible, there are no grounds for ruling out purely physical laws of the same logical form. In addition, given what I believe is a plausible account of the analysis of modal notions – according to which a proposition is logically possible if it is impossible to deduce a contradiction from it using the combination of laws of logic, definitions of terms, and propositions that would generally be viewed as expressing synthetic *a priori* truths – one can show that many propositions that people generally take to be logically possible are in fact so.

Van Inwagen's moral skepticism emerged very clearly with the following statement (2006, 114), which he claimed could be true for all we know:

(3) Being massively irregular is a defect in a world, a defect at least as great as the defect of containing patterns of suffering mentally equivalent to those found in the actual world.

For in explaining what it is for a world to be massively irregular, van Inwagen says that one would have a massively irregular world if "God, by means of an age-long series of ubiquitous miracles, causes a planet inhabited by the same animal life as the actual world to be a hedonic utopia" (2006, 115). So van Inwagen is claiming that if God massively intervened in a world like ours to eliminate undeserved suffering, his doing so would be a defect that was "at least as great" as the totality of all the suffering found in our world. I doubt very much that many people would share this view, including most skeptical theists, who appeal to 'goods beyond our ken' precisely because they think that one cannot specify any state of affairs, such as the absence of ubiquitous miracles, that might, upon reflection, serve as a satisfactory justification for the presence of undeserved suffering.

The question that van Inwagen needs to answer is how one can ever be justified in believing that some particular moral claim is true. One very common answer is that if it seems *intuitively clear to most people, on careful reflection*, that a certain moral principle is true, then one is justified in believing that it is true, and, similarly, if it seems intuitively clear to most people, on careful reflection, that a certain moral principle is false, then one is justified in believing that it is false. If I am right that it would seem to most people that the undeserved suffering endured both by persons and sentient nonpersons is worse than the presence of ubiquitous miracles, then van Inwagen must be viewed as embracing moral skepticism unless he can offer some other, more plausible account of when moral claims are justified.

The third main type of support offered for skeptical theism is that advanced by Michael Bergman. Bergman's central idea appears to be that there is a fundamental principle that determines whether an inductive inference from information about a sample of a given population to a conclusion about the population as a whole is justified. This principle is that such an inference is sound only if we are justified in believing that the sample is *representative*, in the relevant respect, of the population as a whole, where Bergman explains the latter concept as follows: "To say a sample of Xs is representative of all Xs relative to a property F is just to say that if n/m of the Xs in the sample have property F, then approximately n/m of all Xs have F" (2009, 377). Applying this idea to the case at hand, Bergmann advances the following three claims (2009, 376):

ST1: We have no good reason for thinking that the possible goods we know of are representative of the possible goods there are.

ST2: We have no good reason for thinking that the possible evils we know of are representative of the possible evils there are.

ST3: We have no good reason for thinking that the entailment relations we know of between possible goods and the permission of possible evils are representative of the entailment relations there are between possible goods and the permission of possible evils.

Bergmann's approach to inductive reasoning, however, cannot possibly be sound. Suppose that indeed an inference from information about the distribution of some property F within a sample S from some population P to a conclusion about the distribution of property F within population P as a whole is not justified unless one knows that sample S is a *representative* sample with respect to property F within population P. If we then define a representative sample, as Bergmann does, as one where the distribution within sample S approximates the distribution within the population P, then we are in a circle, and inductive inferences from a sample to a population can never be justified. Consequently, the principles to which Bergmann appeals in order to criticize certain arguments from evil against the existence of God – namely, principles ST1, ST2, and ST3 – entail skepticism of a massive kind concerning inductive inferences.

Many subvarieties of these ways of supporting skeptical theism exist, but the time that would be needed to explore those in detail is much better spent in other ways, and this for three reasons. First, as Dougherty points out, the focus of skeptical theists has been exceptionally narrow, as their arguments "were formulated primarily in response to Rowe's arguments" (2016, 3). Thereby two other familiar types of arguments from evil are ignored that, from the get-go, are clearly *much* more promising: those involving abduction, or inference to the best explanation, and those based on fundamental equiprobability principles.

Secondly, the types of argument from evil on which skeptical theists have generally focused – namely, certain ones advanced by William Rowe – either involve, as we shall see, a type of inductive inference that seems clearly unsound, or else, while they employ correct principles of logical probability, contain some premise that a theist can claim, rather plausibly, requires independent support. In either case, the years of labor by skeptical theists to refute such versions of the argument from evil turn out to be time ill spent.

Thirdly, some philosophers have claimed that skeptical theism is exposed to a very serious objection to which skeptical theists have offered no satisfactory response: that skeptical theism leads to skepticism concerning other, vital matters. Is this true?

We have already seen that Michael Bergman's approach is exposed to this objection, while Peter van Inwagen's approach is not only based upon both modal skepticism and moral skepticism, but also leads, for example, to external world skepticism. This is so because if one can defend the view that the suffering of sentient nonhumans does not provide grounds for concluding that it is unlikely that God exists, simply by telling a story that is "true for all anyone knows" (2006, 113) – as van Inwagen claims to do in Lecture 7 in his book *The Problem of Evil* – then one can do the same in defense of Berkeley's view that the only things that exist are an infinite mind and a number of finite minds, and no physical world. For Berkeley's theory generates the same predictions with regard to all of one's sensory experiences as does the theory that the physical world is real, so Berkeley's view could also be "true for all anyone knows."

The same is the case with Stephen Wykstra's attempt to block certain arguments from evil by advancing his 'CORNEA' principle. This is because the latter, as Bruce Russell argues (1988, 148), entails that one is not justified in believing, on the basis of one's sensory experiences, that Descartes' evil demon hypothesis – according to which one's sensory experiences are caused by an evil immaterial being rather than by physical objects – is false.

The crucial question, however, is whether skeptical theism is *necessarily* committed to unacceptable skeptical views. Unfortunately, though many interesting essays have been written on skeptical theism – see, for example, Dougherty and McBrayer (2014) – there has been virtually no discussion of this fundamental question.

How, then, do things stand? First of all, skeptical theism certainly does not entail *universal* skepticism, because the following somewhat vague principle of instantial generalization can be accepted by skeptical theists, since, as we shall see in Section 4.1, it cannot serve as the basis of a sound evidential argument from evil:

> If n F's have been observed – where n is reasonably large – and all of the F's were G's, then it is probable that the next F to be observed will also be a G.

Secondly, however, no principle of instantial generalization can enable one either to justify laws of nature (Tooley 2009, 109–12) or to move from propositions about observable objects to propositions about theoretical entities, since both inferences require either fundamental equiprobability postulates or a principle of inference to the best explanation. The problem then is, as we shall see in Section 4, that both of the latter provide a basis for evidential arguments from evil to which skeptical theists have no answer. The upshot is that skeptical theism can escape from skepticism about laws of nature and about theoretical entities only at the cost of licensing sound evidential arguments from evil.

3.3 What Is the Rationale Behind Appealing to Skeptical *Theism*?

Does skeptical theism at least succeed in refuting incompatibility arguments from evil? This question will be addressed in Section 3.4. First, however, it is worth asking why one would appeal to skeptical *theism* in order to show that incompatibility arguments from evil cannot succeed. Why not simply appeal to the skeptical thesis that is part of skeptical theism?

It is hard to see what the answer is other than that skeptical theists think that belief in the existence of God is rational at least to some extent, thereby lending weight to the idea that there may be unknown goods that justify the evils found in the world.

If something like this is the skeptical theist's underlying line of thought, it is open to the objection that there is no good reason for believing that theism is true. This claim is not uncontroversial, and a thorough defense would require a book in itself. Consider, however, the following. First of all, most arguments offered in support of the existence of God involve no reference to any moral characteristic. The ontological argument is a notable exception, but one can exactly parallel the reasoning involved in any form of that argument and derive contradictions (Tooley, 1981).

Or consider arguments from claimed miracles. Such arguments typically focus on very limited texts, ignoring miracle claims in other texts in the same holy scripture. For example, in the case of Bible-based arguments, no attention is paid to the stories of Noah and the great flood, or Joshua and the battle of Jericho, where we have excellent evidence that the purported and spectacular miracles in question never took place. Arguments from miracles also virtually always ignore information both about the dramatic growth of miracle stories in a short stretch of time. This has been set out, in a detailed and scholarly way in the case of Francis Xavier, by A. D. White 1896, as well as about the failure of any recent and present-day miracle claims to survive critical scrutiny – as shown by the work of D. J. West 1957, Louis Rose 1968, William A. Nolen 1974, James Randi 1987, Joe Nickell 1993, and others, as well as by careful scientific studies, such as the 2005 MANTRA II study (Krucoff et al. 2005) and the 2006 STEP study (Benson et al. 2006).

What about appeals to religious experiences, including ones involving visions and voices, experiences of the 'numinous' (Otto 1958), or theistic mystical experiences? As regards the first, such experiences are strongly tied to the beliefs of the person: Hindu children do not have visions of, nor receive messages from, the Virgin Mary, while Catholic children do not have visions of the Hindu deity, Lord Shiva. As regards the second, numinous experiences do not involve any sense that one is encountering a being that is perfectly good. Finally, as regards theistic mystical experiences, the crucial question is whether theistic mystical experiences have a different ontological basis than the nontheistic introvertive mystical experiences found in Hinduism and Buddhism, and in Plotinus. That question was very carefully investigated by Andrew Robison (1962 and 1973), who examined the descriptions of introvertive mystical experiences given by the monistic mystic Plotinus and Hindu and Buddhist mystics, on the one hand, and, on the other hand, by the theistic mystics Meister Eckhart, St. John of the Cross, and St. Teresa of Avila. Robison's conclusion was that, unless one is oneself a mystic, the most reasonable conclusion, given the total evidence available, is that the references to God that one finds in the descriptions given by the Christian mystics, rather than reflecting any ontologically fundamental features of their experiences differing from those found in nontheistic introvertive mystical experiences, reflect only the conceptual framework that Christian mystics brought to their experiences.

Finally, there is the view, defended by Alvin Plantinga, that not only theism but Christian beliefs are noninferentially justified – are 'properly basic':

> Christian belief is basic; furthermore, Christian belief is *properly* basic, where the propriety in question embraces all three of the epistemic virtues we are considering. On the model, the believer is *justified* in accepting these beliefs in the basic way and is *rational* (both internally and externally) in so doing; still further, the beliefs can have warrant, enough warrant for knowledge, when they are accepted in that basic way. (2000, 259)

There is much to be said concerning the view that religious beliefs are non-inferentially justified and therefore need not be supported by any argument in order to be rational. A thorough consideration would, however, require a long detour through epistemology, so here it will suffice to note that philosophers belonging to non-Christian religions could advance perfectly parallel stories involving an appropriately tailored *sensus divinitatis*, which they then claimed showed that believers in that other religion had warranted beliefs. Once this possibility is on the table, however, how can Christian philosophers, such as Plantinga, be justified in holding that this is the case for members of their own religion, but not for members of other, incompatible religions? Unless these, to all appearances, equally likely possibilities can be shown to be untenable, do they not, first of all, serve as defeaters for Plantinga's claim that humans have a faculty that provides warrant for specifically Christian beliefs, and secondly, also call into question the view that theistic belief is noninferentially justified?

The conclusion, in short, is that if acceptance of skeptical theism is to be justified, it needs to be shown that positive support can be offered for the *theistic* component – something that skeptical theists have failed to do.

3.4 Skeptical Theism and Incompatibility Arguments from Evil: New Work for Skeptical Theists

Skeptical theists generally appear to believe that if the skeptical thesis that is part of skeptical theism is true – that is, if probabilities cannot be assigned to certain propositions about goods and evils beyond our ken – then it follows that no incompatiblity argument from evil can be sound. That view, however, cannot be correct, since it is not enough to claim that there could be goods that lie beyond our ken, the probability of which is unknown: one must also show that those goods *could be connected* with the evils found in this world in such a way that an omnipotent and omniscient being could not obtain those goods without allowing the evils in question. No skeptical theist, however, has shown that this is so.

This general observation is reinforced, moreover, by the incompatibility argument from evil set out earlier, containing as it does a defense of the view that it is impossible for there to be logical connections between goods beyond our ken and certain evils found in this world. This is an argument that involved, first, specifying the conditions under which it would be permissible not to prevent the undeserved suffering of sentient nonpersons when it was within one's power to prevent that suffering, and then, secondly, arguing that those conditions could never obtain for an omnipotent and omniscient person.

How are skeptical theists likely to respond to that argument? Only time will tell. One possibility, however, is clear: one might reject proposition (24):

> The only states of affairs that are intrinsically good or intrinsically bad are ones that involve properties of, or relations between, *conscious* beings, either persons or nonpersons.

Van Inwagen, for example, would presumably reject that proposition, given that, as we have seen, he holds that the world's being massively irregular – something that does not involve properties of, or relations between, conscious beings – is a defect. I think, however, that the vast majority of philosophers working in ethics would accept proposition (24). Consequently, other skeptical theists may very well want to challenge some other step in the argument.

The upshot, in any case, is that skeptical theists have *much* more work to do to justify their claim to have shown that no incompatibility argument from evil is sound. First of all, they need to respond to arguments, including the one set out in Section 2, that can be advanced in support of the claim that there cannot be logical connections of the required kind between, one the one hand, unknown goods and, on the other, certain evils found in this world.

Secondly, more needs to be done than merely responding to particular arguments: skeptical theists need to offer a *positive* argument in support of the claim that there can be logical connections of the required kind.

Finally, skeptical theists need to show that, contrary to what many critics have argued, skeptical theism does not entail unacceptable skeptical consequences. That will require, at the very least, their embracing principles that can be claimed, with at least some plausibility, to enable one to have justified beliefs about an external world, laws of nature, and theoretical entities.

4 Evidential Arguments from Evil

In this section, I shall consider four evidential arguments from evil. The first two are arguments advanced by William Rowe, one appealing to an inductive principle of universal generalization, and the other employing a version of Bayes' theorem. The third argument is then based upon abduction, or inference to the best explanation, and the fourth upon basic equiprobability principles.

4.1 The Argument from Evil and Instantial Generalization

A familiar type of inductive inference is instantial generalization. Here the evidence is a proposition to the effect that everything observed to have property P has turned out to have property Q as well, and the inductively supported conclusion is that the next thing observed to have property P will also have property Q. This '*singular* inductive inference,' where one generalizes from a collection of instances to a further instance, is almost universally accepted.

An extension of this type of inductive reasoning is *universal* inductive inference, where one moves from the premise that everything observed to have property P has also had property Q to the much stronger conclusion that everything that has property P also has property Q. This type of inductive inference is not *universally* accepted, and indeed, I think it can be shown to be unsound. Nevertheless, it is *widely* accepted, since if one holds that laws of nature are simply cosmic regularities, or cosmic regularities that satisfy some further condition, it would seem that at least a crucial part of what justifies a belief that it is a law that everything with property P has property Q is a justified belief that everything that has been observed to have property P has had property Q as well.

4.1.1 William Rowe's Instantial Generalization Argument from Evil

A natural idea, then, and certainly well worth exploring, is whether a sound evidential argument from evil can be constructed using instantial generalization. This type of argument was advanced by William Rowe in his 1991 article, "Ruminations about Evil."

In that article, Rowe formulates the premise of the crucial inference as follows:

> (P) No good state of affairs we know of is such that an omnipotent, omniscient being's obtaining it would morally justify that being's permitting E1 or E2. (1991, 72)

– where "E1" refers to a case of a fawn who dies in a lingering and terrible fashion because of a forest fire, and "E2" to the case of a young girl who is brutally raped, beaten, and murdered.

Commenting on (P), Rowe emphasizes that what proposition (P) says is not simply that we cannot see how various goods would justify an omnipotent, omniscient being's permitting E1 or E2, but rather that

> The good states of affairs I know of, when I reflect on them, meet one or both of the following conditions: either an omnipotent being could obtain them without having to permit either E1 or E2, or obtaining them wouldn't morally justify that being in permitting E1 or E2. (1991, 72)

Rowe then goes on to say that

if this is so, I have reason to conclude that:

(Q) No good state of affairs is such that an omnipotent, omniscient being's obtaining it would morally justify that being's permitting E1 or E2. (1991, 72)

Rowe uses the letter 'J' "to stand for the property a good has just in case obtaining that good would justify an omnipotent, omniscient being in permitting E1 or E2." (1991, 73) When this is done, the above inference can be compactly represented as follows:

(P) No good that we know of has J.

Therefore, probably:

(Q) No good has J.

4.1.2 The Problem with Rowe's Argument

In his article, Rowe, in addressing an objection advanced by Alvin Plantinga, remarks:

In considering the inference from P to Q it is very important to distinguish two criticisms: A. One is entitled to infer Q from P only if she has a good reason to think that if some good had J it would be a good that she knows of. B. One is entitled to infer Q from P only if she has no reason to think that if some good had J it would likely not be a good that she knows of. (1991, 73–74)

Rowe then observes that "Plantinga's criticism is of type A," and since Rowe has argued earlier that this type of criticism leads to inductive skepticism, he concludes that Plantinga's criticism is "not a cogent criticism" (1991, 74). All of this is certainly right; however, there is a different objection that does not lead to inductive skepticism, and which Rowe does not consider.

The objection emerges if one considers something that Rowe says a bit earlier, namely, "If we observe many A's and note that all of them are B's we are justified in believing that the A's we haven't observed are also B's" (1991, 73). The thing to note is that the statement "we are justified in believing that the A's we haven't observed are also B's" can be interpreted in two different ways, either

(1) We are justified in believing that *all* the A's that we haven't observed are also B's.

or

(2) We are justified in believing of *each* of the A's that we haven't observed that that A is also a B.

Here is why this distinction is relevant. On the one hand, Rowe is certainly right that any criticism that claims that one is not justified in inferring (2), unless one has additional information to the effect that unobserved A's are not likely to differ from observed A's with respect to the possession of property B, does entail inductive skepticism. By contrast, this is not so if one rejects, instead, the inference to (1).

Moreover, this is crucial, because it is (1) that Rowe needs, given that the conclusion he is drawing does not concern simply *the next* morally relevant property that someone might consider: conclusion Q asserts, rather, that *all* further morally relevant properties will lack property J. Such a conclusion about all further cases is much stronger than a conclusion about the next case, and one might well think that in some circumstances a conclusion of the latter sort is justified, while a conclusion of the former sort is not.

One way of supporting the latter claim is by arguing (Tooley 1977, 690–3, and 1987, 129–37) that when one is dealing with a generalization that, if it holds, will *not express a law of nature*, the probability that the regularity in question will obtain gets closer and closer to zero, without limit, as the number of potential instances gets larger and larger, and this is so regardless of how large one's evidence base is (Tooley 2009). Is it impossible, then, to justify universal generalizations? The answer is that if laws of nature are more than mere regularities – and, in particular, if they are second-order relations between universals – then the obtaining of a law, and thereby of the corresponding regularity, may have a very high probability upon even quite a small body of evidence. So, universal generalizations can be justified *if* they obtain in virtue of metaphysically underlying, governing laws of nature.

The question, accordingly, is whether, if Q were true, it would express a law – or a consequence of a law. If, as I think is plausible, it would not, then – although it is true that one is justified in holding, of any given, not yet considered, morally relevant property, that *it* is unlikely to have property J – it may very well be that it is *not* probable that *no* goodmaking (or rightmaking) property has property J. It *may*, on the contrary, be probable that there is *some* morally relevant property that does have property J.

This objection could be overcome if one could argue that it is unlikely that there are *many* unknown goodmaking properties. For if the number is small, then the probability that Q is the case may still be high even if Q does not express a law, or a consequence of a law. Moreover, I am inclined to think that it may well be possible to argue that it is unlikely that there are many unknown, morally relevant properties. However, I also think it is very likely that any attempt to establish that conclusion would involve some controversial metaethical claims. Consequently, I think one is justified in concluding that such a line of argument is not, at present, very promising. In any case, unless that can be established, Rowe's argument must be judged to be unsuccessful, and the same will be true of any other attempt to establish the conclusion, *simply via an inductive inference of the universal generalization sort*, that no good exists that is weightier than any evil we know.

4.2 Purely Deductive Probabilistic Arguments from Evil

4.2.1 A Simple Argument

In his 1996 paper, "The Evidential Argument from Evil: A Second Look," William Rowe set aside the problem of attempting to find a satisfactory account of the inductive step involved in direct, inductive formulations of the argument from evil in favor of an argument employing a version of Bayes' theorem. That argument was vigorously criticized by Alvin Plantinga (1998), but Rowe (1998) remained confident that the new argument was sound.

Elsewhere (Tooley 2016, Section 3.4), I have formulated, in a detailed way, an objection to Rowe's argument. What I want to do here, however, is instead to raise a general problem for *any* argument from evil of a deductive probabilistic kind that employs Bayes' theorem, and this can be done by considering the equation in the following proposition:

If $\Pr(\text{God exists}) > 0$ and $\Pr(E) > 0$, then
$$\Pr(\text{God exists}/E) = \frac{\Pr(E/\text{God exists}) \times \Pr(\text{God exists})}{\Pr(E)}$$

Let us consider, then, how one might go about trying to assign values to the three probabilities on the right-hand side of that equation. First of all, suppose that proposition E says simply that the suffering of all of the sentient, nonhuman animals that have ever existed was enormous. Then it would seem eminently reasonable to assign a value very close to one to the probability of proposition E.

What about the other two probabilities? Here things are clearly much more challenging. In the case of the proposition that God exists, one might argue that an omnipotent and omniscient being need not be perfectly good, since it could instead be perfectly evil, or else completely indifferent to good and evil, as the god of deism was. In addition, there are all of the intermediate possibilities between being perfectly good and being morally indifferent to good and evil, and between the latter possibility and being perfectly evil. So unless grounds can be offered for thinking that the purely *a priori* probabilities of these different possibilities are not on a par, one must conclude that the *a priori* probability that a perfectly good, omnipotent, and omniscient being exists must be low – indeed, close to zero. But even if one considers only the first three possibilities, the conclusion will be that the unconditional probability that God exists – that is, the probability that God exists given no evidence at all – is only 1/3.

Finally, what about the value to be assigned to the conditional probability of proposition E, given that God exists? Here a proponent of the present argument might ask, "When you set aside what you know about the actual world, and just consider the idea of a world created by an all-powerful, all-knowing, and perfectly good being, would you not be surprised if it turned out that the world contained intense suffering by an enormous number of sentient beings over a long stretch of time, something that is certainly true in the actual world, given the strong scientific evidence both that mammals experience pain, and that they evolved around 250 million years ago?" But if one does think that that would be surprising, is that not a good reason for assigning a low probability to its being the case that such suffering would exist, given only the proposition that God exists?

4.2.2 The Fundamental Problem with This Type of Argument

The fundamental weakness in deductive probabilistic arguments from evil is connected with the support that is offered for one (or more) of the conditional probability statements involved in the argument. In the simple argument above, there was only one such claim –namely, that the conditional probability of the existence of the suffering in question, given only the proposition that God exists, is low. This was supported by the claim that if one imagines setting aside what one knows about the actual world, and just considers the idea of a world created by an all-powerful, all-knowing, and perfectly good being, one would be surprised if it turned out to contain the enormous amount of suffering that has been endured, for ages, by nonhuman animals.

The problem is that theists can reply, not without some plausibility, that while they would not have expected the suffering described, this is not because they would have expected less suffering. Rather, it is because they would have had no idea at all how much suffering one should expect the world to contain if God existed, and they could add that that is the reasonable view to take.

It may well be that the latter claim can be shown to be incorrect, but if so, that cannot be done using only Bayes' theorem along with other theorems of the purely formal theory of probability. One needs equiprobability principles that enable one to assign *unconditional* probabilities to propositions, which one can then use to determine the conditional probability that the world would contain the enormous amount of suffering that nonhuman animals have endured, for ages, if God existed.

What is true in the case of this simple argument is equally true, I suggest, with deductive probabilistic arguments of a more complex sort that make use of conditional probabilities. Somewhere in the argument there will be a conditional probability claim that a theist can contend, with some plausibility, stands in need of a supporting argument. The latter, however, is something that cannot be provided as long as an appeal is made only to formal principles of probability without advancing any foundational equiprobability principles that would allow one to determine the unconditional probabilities of relevant propositions.

It seems to me, then, that there are good grounds for concluding that deductive probabilistic arguments from evil are not, in the end, promising.

4.3 Abductive Arguments from Evil

4.3.1 The Idea of Abduction

One of the greatest discoveries in philosophy was that there was a method of inductive inference other than that of instantial generalization. This discovery was made by C. S. Peirce, who described abduction as follows in his *Lectures on Pragmatism*, delivered at Harvard in 1903:

> Long before I first classed abduction as an inference it was recognized by logicians that the operation of adopting an explanatory hypothesis – which is just what abduction is – was subject to certain conditions. Namely, the hypothesis cannot be admitted, even as a hypothesis, unless it is supposed that it would account for the facts or some of them. The form of inference, therefore, is this:
>
> The surprising fact, C, is observed.
> But if A were true, C would be a matter of course.
> Hence, there is reason to suspect that A is true. (1955 [1903], 151)

As Peirce says, earlier logicians had described "the operation of adopting an explanatory hypothesis," but they apparently offered no account of when one was justified in concluding that the hypothesis was probably true, and so had not described a method of inference that could serve to justify a belief. Peirce's contribution was that he attempted to do just that, and if one formulates his suggestion using the idea of logical probability and interprets his statement "there is reason to suspect that A is true" as saying that the probability that A is true given C is greater than the initial probability of A, Peirce's proposal can be put as follows:

If the initial probability of C is low, and A entails C, then the probability that A is the case given that C is the case is greater than the initial probability of A.

That this is true can be seen very quickly by using Bayes' theorem, since that gives one:

$$\text{If } \Pr(A) > 0 \text{ and } \Pr(C) > 0, \text{ then } \Pr(A/C) = \frac{\Pr(C/A) \times \Pr(A)}{\Pr(C)}$$

Then, since A entails C, we have that $\Pr(C/A) = 1$, and thus that $\Pr(A/C) = \frac{\Pr(A)}{\Pr(C)}$, and since C is a surprising fact, $\Pr(C)$ must be less than 1, so we have that $\Pr(A/C) > \Pr(A)$.

As one can see, however, this conclusion holds not only when the fact that C is surprising: all that is needed is that the initial probability of C is less than one. Nevertheless, Peirce's focus on cases where the fact that C is surprising captures, in effect, an important fact, namely, that the more improbable C is, the more the relation between A and C will raise the probability that A is the case.

Consider, however, the following. Let C be the fact that John won the lottery, and let A be the proposition that there is an omnipotent being who loves skiing and abhors French philosophy, and who brought it about that John won the lottery. Then John's having won the lottery raises the probability of A, but because the initial probability of A was extremely low, the probability of A given C will still be extremely low, so to say that one then has some reason to suspect that it is true that there is an omnipotent being who loves skiing and abhors French philosophy who brought it about that John won the lottery would be, at best, highly misleading.

The problem here is that an enormous number of propositions have the same logical form as proposition A, but are logically incompatible with A – such as the proposition that there is an omnipotent being who hates skiing, but loves mathematics, who brought it about that John won the lottery. Because of this, proposition A and all related, incompatible propositions will have a very low *a priori* probability of being true. Thus, while C's being true will increase the probability of each of those, the resulting probability of any one is unlikely to be very much greater than the number one divided by the number of such propositions. Consequently, the fact that A entails C, that it is a fact that C, and that it is surprising that C is true, does not necessarily provide a *good reason* for believing that A is probably true.

The conclusion, accordingly, is that for an abductive inference to provide one with a reason for thinking that a proposition A is *likely* to be true, it must *also* be the case that there is no other proposition B whose *a priori* probability is comparable to that of A, and that also entails C.

How widely accepted is the idea of abduction? The answer is that it is quite widely accepted by philosophers. It often goes by other names, however, such as 'the method of hypothesis' as well as 'hypothetico-deductive method' and, perhaps most commonly – and reflecting Peirce's talk about "adopting an explanatory hypothesis" – 'inference to the best explanation.' There is good reason for thinking, therefore, that the idea of formulating an evidential argument from evil that makes use of abduction is not open to the objection that it involves some dubious type of inductive inference – as was the case with arguments employing the principle of universal instantial generalization.

4.3.2 Hume's Discovery

Let us now turn to abductive formulations of the argument from evil. The first formulation of such an argument is found in David Hume's *Dialogues Concerning Natural Religion* – rather surprisingly, since Hume did not have the idea of abduction, and thought of inductive reasoning as always involving an inference from past observed instances of some potential regularity to a conclusion about instances that had not yet been observed. Here, however, is the relevant argument:

> There may *four* hypotheses be framed concerning the first causes of the universe, *that* they are endowed with perfect goodness, *that* they are endowed with perfect malice, *that* they are opposite and have both goodness and malice, *that* they have neither goodness nor malice. Mixed phenomena can never prove the two former unmixed principles. And the uniformity and steadiness of general laws seems to oppose the third. The fourth, therefore, seems by far the most probable. (1779, Part XI, 212)

This passage is preceded by a long discussion by Hume of natural evil, in which he lists four aspects of our world that, on the one hand, are not necessary, but, on the other hand, contribute greatly to the suffering of both humans and other animals, (1779, 205–10), and he concludes, "On the concurrence, then, of these *four* circumstances does all or the greatest part of natural evil depend" (1779, 210). Then after the passage quoted above, Hume also adds, first, that "What I have said concerning natural evil will apply to moral, with little or no variation," and then secondly, that "moral evil, in the opinion of many, is much more predominant above moral good than natural evil above natural good" (1947 [1779], 212).

If Hume's argument is sound, and he is right that the hypothesis that the first cause (or causes) of the universe is neither good nor evil is more probable than any of the other three hypotheses, including the hypothesis that the first cause is perfectly good, then the probability of the latter must be less than one-half.

Hume's statement of his argument, however – in sharp contrast to his extended and detailed discussion of the four circumstances that give rise to suffering – is brief indeed, and could be much more carefully formulated. What is important here, however, is, first, that Hume had moved beyond incompatibility versions of the argument from evil to an evidential argument from evil. Secondly, Hume advanced an evidential argument from evil with a distinct, and interesting, logical form: rather than focusing only on the proposition that the cause of the world is perfectly good and then attempting to show that the facts about evil in the world make it unlikely that that proposition is true, he pointed to other propositions that are logically incompatible with theism. Then he argued that given facts about the goods and evils found in the world, one of those propositions – namely, the hypothesis that the cause or causes of the world "have neither goodness nor malice" – is more probable than the theism hypothesis and, therefore, that theism is more likely to be false than to be true.[1]

4.3.3 Paul Draper and the Biological Function of Pleasure and Pain

Hume's discovery of this type of argument was a very significant achievement. It apparently went unnoticed for a long time, though – perhaps because philosophers were slow to realize that inference to the best explanation is a sound type of inductive argument. More than two centuries later, however, Paul Draper, inspired by Hume, set out and defended this type of inductive argument from evil in a detailed way in his article "Pain and Pleasure: An Evidential Problem for Theists." Draper's approach was to focus on two alternative hypotheses, the first of which he referred to as "the Hypothesis of Indifference," which was as follows (1989, 332):

HI: neither the nature nor the condition of sentient beings on earth is the result of benevolent or malevolent actions performed by nonhuman persons.

Draper then focused upon three sets of propositions about occurrences of pleasure and pain, dealing, respectively, with (a) the experience of pleasure and pain, by moral agents, that is known to be biologically useful, (b) the experience of pleasure and pain, by sentient beings that are not moral agents, that is known to be biologically useful, and (c) the experience of pleasure and pain, by sentient beings, that is not known to be biologically useful. Draper then argued that, where 'O' expresses the conjunction of those three propositions and 'T' expresses the proposition that God exists, the probability of O given HI is greater than the probability of O given T. It then follows – provided that the initial probability of HI is not equal to zero, and that the initial probability of T is not greater than that of HI – that T is more likely to be false than to be true.

---

[1] For a fuller account of Hume's argument, see Tooley (2011).

The crucial part of Draper's argument involves establishing that the probability that O is the case given HI is greater than the probability of O given T. How does Draper tackle that task? The answer is as follows (1989, 334):

> The claim that P(O/HI) is much greater than P(O/theism) is by no means obviously true. The fact that O reports observations and testimony about pleasure as well as pain should make this clear. So an argument for this claim is needed. I will argue that it is the biological role played by both pain and pleasure in goal-directed organic systems that renders this claim true.

The argument that Draper sets out is very detailed, but a key part of it is as follows (1989, 336–7):

> So theism entails both that God does not need biologically useful pain and pleasure to produce human goal-directed organic systems and that, if human pain and pleasure exist, then God had good moral reasons for producing them, reasons that, for all we know antecedently, might very well be inconsistent with pain and pleasure systematically contributing to the biological goals of human organisms. Therefore, we would have much less reason on theism than on HI to be surprised if it turned out that human pain and pleasure differed from other parts of organic systems by not systematically contributing to the biological goals of those systems.

This is an interesting argument; it does not, however, take the idea of skeptical theism into account. This is no fault of Draper's, since virtually all the literature defending skeptical theism was published after Draper's article. The point, nevertheless, is that a skeptical theist can respond by arguing that – given the existence of goods and evils beyond our ken, and which may, for all we know, be logically connected with the fact that pleasure and pain serve biological purposes – we cannot assign *any specific* probability at all to O given theism, which entails that one is not justified in claiming that the probability of O given HI is higher than the probability of O given theism.

4.3.4 Trent Dougherty's Discovery: A Crucial Supplementation of Draper's Abductive Argument from Evil

The criticism just made, which is similar to one put forward by Michael Bergmann (2009, 383ff.), might well seem to block abductive arguments from evil of the kind advanced by Hume and Draper by undercutting any argument in support of premises such as the following:

> 1. The distribution of suffering in the world is more to be expected on naturalism than theism. (Dougherty, 2016, 34)

Trent Dougherty has shown, however, that that is not the case: one can *supplement* any argument that appeals to Draper-style considerations of facts concerning pleasure and pain in the world by a new argument to establish the *conditional* result that, even if the skeptical claim involved in skeptical theism is *true*, the Hypothesis of Indifference is still more probable than theism. Draper's original argument can then be viewed as establishing the *conditional* conclusion that if the skeptical claim involved in skeptical theism is *false*, then the Hypothesis of Indifference is more probable than theism. The two arguments combined then give one an abductive argument from evil that is not open to a skeptical theist objection.

Here is how Dougherty (2016, 35) sets out his argument:

> Skeptical theism attempts to block Premise 1 of the above argument by blocking an assignment of probability to observed evil on theism. However, consider this reformulation. Given: The universe seems indifferent to the suffering of sentient beings.
>
> 1'. It is known that the hypothesis of indifference predicts the data of an apparently indifferent universe.
> 2. It is unknown whether the hypothesis of theism predicts the data.
> 3. The hypotheses have approximately equal prior probabilities [that is, equal chance of being true before considering observational evidence].
> 4. Therefore, the data confirm the hypothesis of indifference and not the hypothesis of theism.

This is an interesting and promising argument, at the heart of which is a point that no one else seems to have noticed; however, Dougherty did not formulate his argument as tightly as he could have, with the result that Daniel Howard-Snyder, in a rather vigorous article, "How Not to Render an Explanatory Version of the Evidential Argument from Evil Immune to Skeptical Theism" (2015), attempted to show that Dougherty's argument was without merit. Howard-Snyder, however, failed to grasp the point that lies at the heart of Dougherty's argument, resulting, in the end, in a long series of criticisms that do not bear upon *the core idea*, and consequently, criticisms that become irrelevant when Dougherty's argument is formulated in a more circumspect way. Accordingly, let me recast Dougherty's argument so that it is not open to such objections. First, it will be helpful to use some abbreviations:

Theism (T): There is an omnipotent, omniscient, and perfectly good being who created everything, including the physical universe and its laws.

The Hypothesis of Indifference (HI): Neither the universe nor its laws nor sentient beings were the result of benevolent or malevolent actions performed by nonhuman persons.

The Laws of the Physical Universe are Not Sensitive to the Well-Being of Humans or other Sentient Beings (NSW): The laws of the physical universe involve no reference to either the well-being or the suffering of humans or other sentient beings.

The Skeptical Thesis that is Part of Skeptical Theism (ST): Religious knowledge aside, we have no grounds for assigning probabilities to propositions concerning goods or evils that may exist beyond our ken.

Dougherty's argument can now be put a little more expansively as follows:

1. The *a priori* probability of the Hypothesis of Indifference is equal to the *a priori* probability of theism:

(1) $\Pr(\text{HI}) = \Pr(\text{T})$.

2. The probability that the laws of the physical universe are insensitive to the well-being of humans or other sentient beings is higher given the Hypothesis of Indifference than it is initially:

(2) $\Pr(\text{NSW}/\text{HI}) > \Pr(\text{NSW})$.

3. By Bayes' Theorem,

(3) $\Pr(\text{HI}/\text{NSW}) = \dfrac{Pr(\text{NSW}/\text{HI}) \times \Pr(\text{HI})}{\Pr(\text{NSW})}$

4. It then follows from (2) and (3) that

(4) $\Pr(\text{HI}/\text{NSW}) > \dfrac{Pr(\text{NSW}) \times \Pr(\text{HI})}{\Pr(\text{NSW})}$

By cancellation of $\Pr(\text{NSW})$ we then have that

(5) $\Pr(\text{HI}/\text{NSW}) > \Pr(\text{HI})$.

5. It then follows from (1) and (5) that

(6) $\Pr(\text{HI}/\text{NSW}) > \Pr(\text{T})$

6. If the skeptical thesis involved in skeptical theism is true, we do not know the value of $\Pr(\text{NSW}/\text{T})$, *so information about how that probability compares with* $\Pr(\text{NSW})$ *cannot be part of our total evidence.*

7. Accordingly, if the skeptical thesis involved in skeptical theism is true, our *total relevant evidence* consists of the following: $\Pr(\text{HI}) = \Pr(\text{T})$, and $\Pr(\text{HI}/\text{NSW}) > \Pr(\text{T})$

8. If the skeptical thesis involved in skeptical theism is true, then given our total evidence, the rational belief is that the Hypothesis of Indifference is more probable than theism.

Thus reformulated, the resulting argument, though incorporating Draper's work, differs dramatically from Draper's argument. Rather than comparing the probabilities of *two competing explanations* of the absence, in the laws of the physical universe, of any reference to the well-being or the suffering of humans or other sentient beings, it aims instead at showing that *if* the skeptical thesis involved in skeptical theism is *true*, then it is rational to believe that the Hypothesis of Indifference is more probable than theism. Then, if a Draper-style argument succeeds in showing that *if* the skeptical thesis involved in skeptical theism is *false*, the Hypothesis of Indifference is more probable than theism, the two arguments taken together constitute a sound abductive argument from evil that cannot be undercut by skeptical theism.

Dougherty's argument is thus a novel and an extremely important contribution to philosophical discussion of abductive arguments from evil.

4.4 Logical Probability and Fundamental Equiprobability Principles

Aside from necessary truths and necessary falsehoods, whose *a priori* logical probabilities are equal, respectively, to one and zero, one cannot determine the *a priori* logical probability of any other proposition without appealing to equiprobability principles. But what is an equiprobability principle? Basically, equiprobability principles simply say that propositions that are related in certain specified ways have *the same a priori* logical probability. Here are two widely accepted equiprobability principles.

Equiprobability Principle 1: Families of Properties

If properties F and G belong to a family of properties, where a family of properties is a set of mutually exclusive and jointly exhaustive properties, all either basic properties or else structurally the same at every level, then the *a priori* probability that x has property F is equal to the *a priori* probability that x has property G.

As an illustration, consider the family of fully determinate color properties. Equiprobability Principle 1 then says that if F and G are any two completely determinate colors, the probability, given no further information, that some particular object x has property F is equal to the probability that x has property G.

Equiprobability Principle 2: The Interchange of Individuals

If x and y are any two nonoverlapping individuals, and F is any property that involves no reference to either individual x or individual y, then the *a priori* probability that x has property F is equal to the *a priori* probability that y has property F.

The crucial point is now that it is possible to formulate arguments from evil that, rather than appealing either to the ideas of singular or universal inductive inference, or to that of abductive inference, appeal *only* to equiprobability principles.

4.5 Equiprobability-Based Evidential Arguments from Evil: An Overview

Two basic points. First, evidential arguments from evil should *ultimately* be formulated using *fundamental* equiprobability principles. Secondly, equiprobability-based arguments from evil can have either of two very different starting points: one focuses initially on single *prima facie* evils; the other starts instead with some general proposition about evils found in the world.

As regards the first point, the argument I shall set out involves two parts, the first concerned with the probability that God exists, given a single evil, and the second with the probability given multiple evils. The first part requires only a single equiprobability principle, namely Equiprobability Principle 1, concerning families of properties – a principle that is almost always part of any system of logical probability.

The second part, in the version I now believe is correct, uses an equiprobability principle that is not, in my opinion, fundamental – namely, that as regards what are known as state-descriptions, all relevant ones have the same *a priori* probability. It is widely believed, however, due to an argument advanced by Rudolf Carnap (1962, 565), that that principle cannot be right, on the grounds that it entails that one cannot learn from experience. It can be shown, however, not only that Carnap's argument is unsound, but also that his conclusion is false: a state-description equiprobability principle *does* enable one to learn from experience.

As regards the second point, while I shall not set out the alternative type of evidential argument from evil that starts instead from some *general* proposition about the *prima facie* evils found in the world, I shall briefly describe, in Section 4.5.2, why I think that a Draper-style argument could be formulated without using the idea of abduction by employing, instead, fundamental equiprobability principles.

4.5.1 A Simple, Prima Facie *Argument for Atheism: Atheism as the Default Position*

In Section 4.6, I shall set out what I believe is the most fundamental type of evidential argument from evil. First, however, I think it will be helpful to set out a simpler argument for atheism, based upon the same equiprobability principle used in the part of my argument concerned with the probability that God exists given the existence of a single *prima facie* evil.

Incompatibility arguments from evil, if sound, prove that an omnipotent, omniscient, and morally perfectly good being cannot exist. Evidential arguments, however, if sound, show only that, given certain facts about evils, it is unlikely that God exists, unless there is positive support for the existence of God of sufficient strength to counterbalance the negative evidence provided by existing evils. The simple argument for atheism that follows is similar, since the conclusion is also merely that the existence of God is unlikely in the absence of positive support for the existence of God.

In contrast to evidential arguments from evil, however, the probability claim involved in the simple argument does not appeal to *any facts about the world* that are negative evidence against the existence of God: the claim is instead that the existence of God is *a priori* unlikely.

Here, then, is the argument, a version of which I offered previously in the debate volume, *Knowledge of God*, coauthored with Alvin Plantinga (2008, 90–3):

(1) For an omnipotent and omniscient being to be God, that being must also be perfectly good.

(2) The property of being perfectly good is one member of *a family of properties* covering the moral character that an omnipotent and omniscient being might have, two other members of which are (a) the property of being perfectly evil, and (b) the property of being completely indifferent between performing morally right actions and performing morally wrong actions.

(3) There are, however, other members of that family, since one can be morally good to various degrees lying between being morally indifferent to good and evil and being perfectly good. Similarly, one can be morally evil to various degrees between being morally indifferent to good and evil and being perfectly evil. Arguably, the number of such possibilities may be infinite, but, for simplicity, let us suppose that there are n different possibilities.

(4) Equiprobability Principle 1 says that given any two members of a family of properties, the *a priori* probability of some individual thing's having the first property is equal to the *a priori* probability of its having the second property.

(5) It follows that if a family of properties has n members, then for any property, P, belonging to that family, the *a priori* probability that a given individual has property P is equal to $1/n$.

(6) It then follows from (3) and (5) that if there is an omnipotent and omniscient being, the *a priori* probability that that being has the property of being perfectly good is equal to $1/n$.

(7) There is also some nonzero *a priori* probability that there is *no* omnipotent and omniscient being of any kind, in which case God would not exist.

(8) It follows from (6) and (7) that the *a priori* probability that God exists is less than $1/n$.

In response, one might try to undercut this conclusion by claiming that the intermediate properties between being perfectly good and being indifferent to good and evil, and between the latter and being perfectly evil should be assigned less weight than the three central properties – though I think it very unlikely that any such argument exists. Moreover, even if such an argument did exist, given the three remaining central properties, it would still follow that the probability that God exists, even assuming that there is an omnipotent and omniscient being, cannot be greater than $1/3$, so the nonexistence of God would still be substantially more probable than the existence of God.

Another possible response is that this conclusion is not really very threatening, since many positive arguments can be offered in support of the existence of God, and surely not much is needed to overthrow the force of this purely *a priori* argument. This response, however, overlooks the fact that almost all the arguments advanced, allegedly supporting the existence of *God*, are in fact arguments that do not bear upon *the moral character* of the being in question. To overcome the present argument, one needs to find sound arguments for the existence of a *perfectly good* deity; however, as was argued earlier in Section 3.3, the prospects for doing that do not seem promising.

4.5.2 Possible Alternatives with Regard to Equiprobability Evidential Arguments from Evil

As regards morally significant properties of actions, let us say that a property is a *rightmaking* property if an action's possessing that property, and no other morally significant property, entails that one should perform the action, and that a property is a *wrongmaking* property if an action's possessing that property, and no other morally significant property, entails that one should not perform the action.

Some morally significant properties, however, are more significant than others, so such properties must have different weights – positive weights for rightmaking properties, and negative weights for wrongmaking properties. The moral status of an action will then be given by the sum of the weights of all the rightmaking and wrongmaking properties of the action.

Next, one needs to distinguish between an action's being morally right or morally wrong as judged by the rightmaking and wrongmaking properties of which one is aware, and an action's being right or wrong as judged by the totality of rightmaking and wrongmaking properties that exist, *both known and unknown*. Judged by the rightmaking properties and wrongmaking properties of which humans are aware, an action of not preventing the influenza epistemic of 1918, when one could have done so, would have been wrong – indeed, heinously so. It is possible, however – as skeptical theists would insist – that there may be rightmaking or wrongmaking properties of which we humans are not aware, such that judged by the *totality* of rightmaking and wrongmaking properties, both known and unknown, an omnipotent and omniscient being who did not intervene to prevent that epidemic would have acted rightly.

In what follows, the question will frequently arise as to whether propositions about actions that are morally wrong as judged by the rightmaking and wrongmaking properties of which one is aware have a bearing upon the probabilities of propositions about actions being right or wrong as judged by the totality of rightmaking and wrongmaking properties that exist, both known and unknown. Given that the statements I have just used to express the two types of propositions in question are rather wordy, it will be good to have a more succinct way of expressing that distinction. To do that, I shall use the expressions "a *prima facie* evil" and "an *all things considered* evil" as follows:

"State of affairs S is a *prima facie* evil."

means the same as

"State of affairs S is such that any action of failing to prevent the existence of S when one could have done so, without cost or danger to oneself, is, as judged in the light of *our present knowledge* of the rightmaking and wrongmaking properties of actions, morally wrong."

"State of affairs S is an *all things considered* evil."

means the same as

"State of affairs S is such that any action of failing to prevent the existence of S when one could have done so, without cost or danger to oneself, is, as judged in the light of *the totality* of the rightmaking and wrongmaking properties of actions, *both known to us and unknown to us*, morally wrong."

Next, consider the choice when one is setting out an evidential argument from evil based on one or more equiprobability principles. On the one hand, one can begin by focusing on *individual prima facie* evils and attempt to determine how likely it is that such *prima facie* evils are also *all things considered* evils. The goal here would be to show that, given any single *prima facie* evil, the probability that that evil is also an *all things considered* evil is greater than one-half.

An omnipotent and omniscient being would be able to prevent any *all things considered* evil, so the failure of such a being to do so would be morally wrong. Such a being would therefore not be morally perfect, and thus would not be God, if God is a being that is omnipotent, omniscient, and morally perfect.

The existence of a single, *all things considered* evil therefore entails the nonexistence of God. The following, however, is a theorem of the formal theory of probability:

If the probability of p, given e, is greater than k, and p entails q, then the probability of q, given e, is also greater than k.

This gives us the following:

Proposition 1: The Probability of God and the Probability of a Single *All Things Considered* Evil

If the probability, given a *prima facie* evil, that it is an *all things considered* evil, is greater than k, then the probability that God does not exist, given that *prima facie* evil, is also greater than k.

If one could prove that, given any single *prima facie* evil, the probability – call it k_1 – that that evil was also an *all things considered* evil, was greater than one-half, one would then like to determine the probability – call it k_2 – that if there were two *prima facie* evils, at least one of those would be an *all things considered* evil, with the initial goal being to show that k_2 is greater than k_1.

Finally, one would also like to prove that, as the number, n, of *prima facie* evils increases without limit, the probability – k_n – that at least one of those *prima facie* evils was an *all things considered* evil approaches the value one as n increases without limit, thus entailing that the probability that God does not exist also approaches the value one, so that the probability that God does exist approaches the value zero.

This type of equiprobability-based evidential argument is, I believe, the most fundamental kind, starting as it does with a single evil, and then going on to consider multiple evils. However, while the case of a single evil is straightforward, the extension to two or more evils is more challenging, and it turns out that, even if one knows how to calculate the probability k_n for any value of n, it is not easy to find a mathematical formula that generates the probability for every value of n. In addition, it is possible that even if one has succeeded in deriving the general formula, finding the limit of the value of k_n as n goes to infinity may not be a trivial exercise.

Finally, it is worth considering whether there can be another type of equiprobability-based evidential argument from evil that, rather than focusing on a single evil, starts instead from some general fact about evils found in the world, and then attempts to show that one or more equiprobability principles entail the result that the probability that God exists, given the general fact in question, is less than one-half – and perhaps much less than one-half. I cannot explore this question here, but I think it likely that such an argument is possible. My reason is that abduction, or inference to the best explanation, is not a plausible candidate for a *basic* principle of induction, and, if that is so, it must be derived from fundamental equiprobability principles. If that can be done, one could recast a Draper-style argument, starting, perhaps, with the proposition that the extent to which people suffer appears to be unrelated to how they are morally as people, and then using equiprobability principles to show that the Hypothesis of Indifference is more likely to be true than theism is. The result would then be a Draper-style argument to which skeptical theism was no longer an objection in view of the general equiprobability principles, so there would be no need to supplement a Draper-style argument with Trent Dougherty's argument. This seems to me, at the very least, a promising research project.

4.6 The Most Fundamental Equiprobability-Based Evidential Argument from Evil: From Single Evils to Multiple Evils

4.6.1 The Case of a Single Evil – the Underlying Idea

Let E be some *prima facie* evil – such as Rowe's case of the five-year-old girl who is brutally beaten, raped, and murdered – and let A be an action of not preventing E when one could have done so at no cost or danger to oneself. Judged by the rightmaking and wrongmaking properties of which we are aware, action A is seriously wrong. Suppose, however, that there are two unknown morally significant properties that are equally weighty, one rightmaking, and the other wrongmaking, which action A may or may not possess, and where both of those unknown properties are weightier than the totality of the known wrongmaking properties of action A.

We now need to consider the different possibilities that exist, and to represent those possibilities in a perspicuous way, I shall use the following type of diagram:

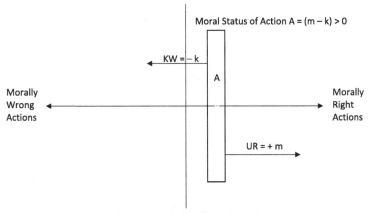

Known Morally Significant Properties

Moral Status of Action A = (m − k) > 0

KW = − k

A

Morally Wrong Actions

Morally Right Actions

UR = + m

Unknown Morally Significant Properties

Here, action A is represented by a rectangle, and arrows attached to A represent *rightmaking* or *wrongmaking* properties, depending on the direction in which they point. Arrows above the horizontal axis represent *known* rightmaking and wrongmaking properties, while those below represent *unknown* rightmaking and wrongmaking properties. Finally, action A is *morally permissible* as judged by *the totality* of its rightmaking and wrongmaking properties, both known and unknown, when A is to the right of the vertical line, and *morally impermissible* when it is to the left of that line.

Accordingly, the diagram above says that action A has one known wrongmaking property of magnitude k, no known rightmaking properties, one unknown rightmaking property of magnitude m, and no unknown wrongmaking properties. The unknown rightmaking property is weightier than the known wrongmaking property, with the result that action A is an action that one should perform if one's knowledge of rightmaking and wrongmaking properties were complete.

Consider, now, the simple case mentioned above, where action A has one known wrongmaking property and no known rightmaking properties, and where the world contains two *equally weighty, unknown* morally significant properties – a rightmaking property UR and a wrongmaking property UW – either or both of which any given action may or may not have, and where these unknown morally significant properties are each weightier than the total of the known wrongmaking properties that A possesses. There are, accordingly, the following four possibilities:

Possibility 1: Action A does not possess either the unknown rightmaking property UR or the unknown wrongmaking property UW;

Possibility 2: Action A possesses property UR, but not property UW;

Possibility 3: Action A possesses property UW, but not property UR;

Possibility 4: Action A possesses both properties, UR and UW.

Here is a diagram that represents the first possibility:

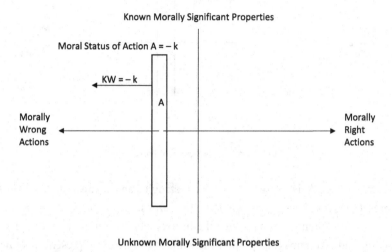

Diagram 1 – Possibility 1: Neither UR nor UW is present.

If this is how things are, then action A is an action that is morally wrong all things considered, that is, given the totality of rightmaking and wrongmaking properties, both known and unknown.

Next, here is a diagram representing the second possibility:

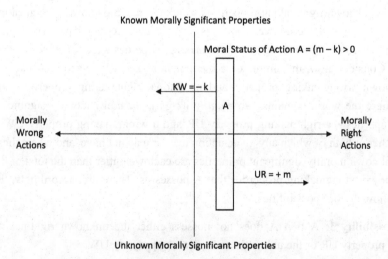

Diagram 2 – Possibility 2: UR is present, but not UW.

If this is how things are, then action A is an action that is morally right all things considered, since the unknown rightmaking property that action A has is weightier than the known wrongmaking property KW that A possesses.

Here is the third possibility:

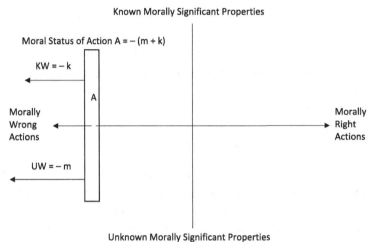

Diagram 3 – Possibility 3: UW is present, but not UR.

If this is how things are, then action A is an action that is morally wrong all things considered, and more seriously wrong than it is relative to its known wrongmaking property since it also has the unknown wrongmaking property UW, but not the unknown rightmaking property UR.

Here is the fourth and final possibility:

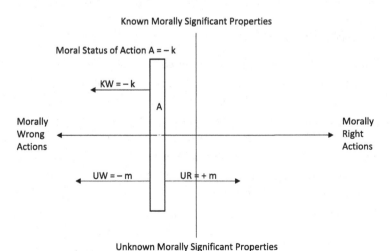

Diagram 4 – Possibility 4: Both UR and UW are present

If this is how things are, then action A is an action that is morally wrong all things considered since, on the one hand, it has a known wrongmaking property; on the other hand, while it does have the unknown rightmaking property UR, it also has the equally weighty unknown wrongmaking property UW, so that it is morally wrong given the totality of morally significant properties that it possesses.

What is the conclusion in this special case with one apparent evil, in a world with two unknown and equally significant morally significant properties, one rightmaking and the other wrongmaking? The answer is that since, in three of the four possibilities set out in Diagrams 1 through 4, action A is morally wrong all things considered, action A is three times as likely to be morally wrong as to be morally permissible.

4.6.2 Step One: The Case of a Single Prima Facie Evil

In the illustration, it turned out that an action that was wrong as judged by known rightmaking and wrongmaking properties was also wrong as judged by the totality of rightmaking and wrongmaking properties, both known and unknown; however, this resulted from the fact that there were only two unknown, equally weighty morally significant properties, one of which was rightmaking, and the other wrongmaking. We now need to see how the result in this special case can be generalized.

The key to doing that is Equiprobability Principle 1, from Section 4.4, concerning families of properties:

> If properties F and G belong to a family of properties, where a family of properties is a set of mutually exclusive and jointly exhaustive properties, all either basic properties or else structurally the same at every level, then the *a priori* probability that *x* has property F is equal to the *a priori* probability that *x* has property G.

Consider, now, the following *second-order property* of properties: that of being a rightmaking property of weight *x*. That property is logically incompatible with the second-order property of being a *wrongmaking* property of weight *x*. Those two second-order properties are also structurally the same, so they belong to a family of properties. It therefore follows from Equiprobability Principle 1 that, for any *x*, the *a priori* probability that a given property P has the second-order property of being a rightmaking property of weight *x* is equal to the *a priori* probability that property P has the second-order property of being a wrongmaking property of weight *x*.

Consider, then, some *prima facie* evil S. What are the possibilities with regard to relevant *unknown* rightmaking and wrongmaking properties of the action of not preventing the existence of S? One possibility is that there are no relevant unknown rightmaking and wrongmaking properties. In that case, S will be an *all things considered* evil. A second possibility is that there are relevant unknown rightmaking properties, but no relevant unknown wrongmaking properties. In that case, S will not be an *all things considered* evil *provided that* the relevant unknown rightmaking properties outweigh the known wrongmaking property, but will be an *all things considered* evil if they do not. A third possibility is that there are relevant unknown wrongmaking properties, but no relevant unknown rightmaking properties. In that case, S will be an *all things considered* evil. The final possibility is that there are both relevant unknown rightmaking properties and unknown wrongmaking properties. Then – given that, for any property P and any weight x, the *a priori* likelihood that P has the property of being a rightmaking property of weight x is equal to the *a priori* probability that P has the property of being a wrongmaking property of weight x – for every case where some collection of relevant unknown rightmaking properties outweighs a collection of relevant unknown wrongmaking properties, there will be a completely parallel and equally probable case where an exactly corresponding collection of relevant unknown wrongmaking properties outweighs a collection of relevant unknown rightmaking properties. But there will also be cases where, although some collection of relevant unknown rightmaking properties outweighs a collection of relevant unknown wrongmaking properties, the collection of relevant unknown rightmaking properties does not outweigh *the combination* of the collection of relevant unknown wrongmaking properties with the *known* wrongmaking properties.

The conclusions, accordingly, are as follows:

(1) When there are no relevant unknown rightmaking or wrongmaking properties, S will be an *all things considered* evil;

(2) The number of cases falling under the third possibility, where there are relevant unknown wrongmaking properties but no relevant unknown rightmaking properties, so that S will be an *all things considered* evil, is greater than the number of cases falling under the second possibility, where there are relevant unknown rightmaking properties but no relevant unknown wrongmaking properties, *and where* the unknown rightmaking properties outweigh the known wrongmaking property, so that S will *not* be an *all things considered* evil;

(3) When there are both relevant unknown rightmaking properties and relevant unknown wrongmaking properties, the number of cases in which S will be an *all things considered* evil is greater than the number of cases in which S will not be an *all things considered* evil, since the unknown rightmaking properties may not outweigh the known wrongmaking property.

In view of (1), (2), and (3), then, we have the following conclusion:

Conclusion 1: The Case of a Single *Prima Facie* Evil

If S is a *prima facie* evil, the probability that S will be an *all things considered* evil is greater than ½.

Recall now Proposition 1, set out above in Section 4.5.2:

If the probability, given a *prima facie* evil, that it is an *all things considered* evil, is greater than k, then the probability that God does not exist, given that *prima facie* evil, is also greater than k.

This, together with Conclusion 1, then entails:

Conclusion 2: The Relevance of a Single Evil to the Existence of God

If S is a *prima facie* evil, then the probability that God exists, given S, is less than ½.

4.6.3 Step Two: The Case of Multiple Prima Facie Evils

Next, what happens to the probability that God exists when there is more than one *prima facie* evil? Since the existence of even a single *all things considered* evil is incompatible with the existence of God, the probability that God exists cannot be greater than the probability that, of all the *prima facie* evils found in the world, *not even one* of those is an *all things considered* evil. In addition, given that the probability that God exists given a single *prima facie* evil is less than one-half, and given the extraordinary number of *prima facie* evils in the world, it would be quite surprising if it turned out that the probability that God exists, given the *prima facie* evils there are in the world, was not very low indeed.

How can one calculate that probability? To understand the possible answers to that question, a crucial distinction is needed: that between *state-descriptions* and *structure-descriptions*. Consider an urn that contains ten marbles, all of which are either red or green. Here a state-description would specify the color of *each marble*, so the statement that marbles 1, 3, 4, and 8 are red, while marbles 2, 5, 6, 7, 9, and 10 are green, is a state-description. A structure-description, by contrast, would tell only *how many* marbles were red, and *how many* were green, and so would not tell, of any of the ten marbles, what color *that* marble was – except when the structure-description is either that all ten marbles are red, or that all ten are green.

Some philosophers, including C. S. Pierce (1932 [1883], 470 f.), John Maynard Keynes (1921, 56–57), and Ludwig Wittgenstein (1922, *5.15), held that all state-descriptions applying to a given situation are equally probable. So, in the case of the urn, the state-description according to which marbles 1 through 9 are all red, while marble 10 is green, would have the same *a priori* probability as the state-description according to which marbles 1 through 10 are all red. Laplace (1812) and Carnap (1962, 565), on the other hand, held instead that all structure-descriptions (or proportions) were equally likely. This entails that the state-description according to which marbles 1 through 10 are all red has an *a priori* probability that is ten times that of the state-description according to which marbles 1 through 9 are all red, while marble 10 is green, since the former state-description is equivalent to the structure-description that all ten marbles are red, whereas the latter is just one of ten state-descriptions falling under the structure-description that nine of the ten marbles are red, and the other one green.

Suppose, now, that there are N *prima facie* evils. What are the probabilities that at least one of those *prima facie* evils is an *all things considered* evil, given, on the one hand, a state-description equiprobability assumption and, on the other, a structure-description equiprobability assumption?

Before setting out what I now take to be the right approach, let me describe the approach that I followed earlier, both when one assumes that state-descriptions are equally likely, and when one assumes that structure-descriptions are equally likely.

In the case of a state-description equiprobability assumption, the answer was arrived at as follows (Plantinga and Tooley 2008, 150). Given the above result, in the case of a single *prima facie* evil, that the probability that that *prima facie* evil is an *all things considered* evil is less than $\frac{1}{2}$, the probability that none of those N *prima facie* evils is an *all things considered* evil must be less than $\left(\frac{1}{2}\right)^{N}$. So, for example, given ten *prima facie* evils, the probability that none of them is an *all things considered* evil is less than $\left(\frac{1}{2}\right)^{10}$, which is slightly less than one chance in a thousand.

In the case of a structure-description equiprobability assumption, carrying out the calculation is rather more challenging. But an argument that I set out, first in the co-authored *Knowledge of God* debate volume (Plantinga and Tooley, 2008, 135–150), and then, in a slightly different way, in "Inductive Logic and the Probability that God Exists: Farewell to Skeptical Theism" (Tooley 2012), generated the result that the probability in question is less than $\frac{1}{N+1}$.

I now have, however, new methods – which I think are superior – for carrying out both calculations, and which I arrived at by thinking about the following possible objection to the previous methods:

> Both the state-description and the structure-description calculations do not seem to consider the possibility that there is a *single* extremely weighty

rightmaking consideration that applies to multiple *prima facie* evils, and that
makes it morally permissible to allow all of those *prima facie* evils. May it not
be that, when this possibility is taken into account, the probability that God
exists is not as low as it is according to the previous calculations?

This is a thought that should certainly have occurred to me initially.
Theodicies and defenses often try to argue that God is justified in allowing the
totality of natural evils because of the great good of having natural laws, as
Richard Swinburne (1998, 182–98) contended, or because of the for-all-we-
know possibility, as in Peter van Inwagen's defense, that "Being massively
irregular is a defect in a world, a defect at least as great as the defect of
containing patterns of suffering mentally equivalent to those found in the actual
world" (2006, 114).

I argued above that such claims are implausible. The point here, however, is
simply that the claim that one can *specify* either some great good that outweighs known multiple evils, or some purportedly greater evil that can only be
avoided by allowing many other evils, can be replaced by the claim that it is
possible either that there is some unknown good that outweighs multiple evils
in our world, and for which those evils are necessary, or that there is some
unknown evil that can only be avoided by allowing multiple evils found in our
world.

I therefore concluded that my earlier methods needed to be revised in view
of this point. So how can one carry out the calculations to take this possibility
into account? First of all, it will simplify the calculation if we set aside the
following two possibilities: one is that that there are no unknown rightmaking
or wrongmaking properties at all; the other is that, for some *prima facie* evils,
there are no relevant unknown rightmaking or wrongmaking properties.
(Doing this will generate a *higher* estimate of the probability that none of
the *prima facie* evils is an *all things considered* evil and thus is clearly
unobjectionable.)

Let us consider, then, each of the two equiprobability principles in turn,
starting with the assumption that all *structure-descriptions* are equally probable.
To illustrate the general idea, let us suppose that there are only three *prima facie*
evils. One then has the following three structure-descriptions, each with an *a
priori* probability of $\frac{1}{3}$:

Structure-description 1: All three *prima facie* evils are related to a single,
unknown, morally significant property – which may be either a rightmaking
property or a wrongmaking property.

Structure-description 2: Two of the *prima facie* evils are related to a single,
unknown, morally significant property, while the other *prima facie* evil is

related to a different, unknown, morally significant property – each of which may be either rightmaking or wrongmaking.

Structure-description 3: All three *prima facie* evils are related to different, unknown, morally significant properties – each of which may be either rightmaking or wrongmaking.

In the case of structure-description 1, the unknown morally significant property in question may be either rightmaking or wrongmaking – each of which is equally probable – so that if structure-description 1 obtains, the probability that the property in question is a rightmaking property is equal to $\frac{1}{2}$.

One also needs to factor in, however, what can be called the 'counterbalancing failure' – the possibility that, while the morally significant property is rightmaking rather than wrongmaking, it is *not sufficiently weighty* to counterbalance the known wrongmaking property. Consequently, if structure-description 1 obtains, the *a priori* probability that none of the *prima facie* evils are *all things considered* evils must be *less than* $\frac{1}{2}$.

In the case of structure-description 2, the unknown morally significant property related to two of the *prima facie* evils may be either rightmaking or wrongmaking. The same is true of the different, unknown, morally significant property related to the other *prima facie* evil, so if structure-description 2 obtains, and taking into account the two 'counterbalancing failure' possibilities, the *a priori* probability that none of the *prima facie* evils are *all things considered* evils must be less than $\left(\frac{1}{2} \times \frac{1}{2}\right)$, and thus *less than* $\frac{1}{4}$.

Finally, in the case of structure-description 3, the three unknown morally significant properties related to the three *prima facie* evils may be either right-making or wrongmaking, so if structure-description 3 obtains, and taking into account the three 'counterbalancing failure' possibilities, the *a priori* probability that none of the three *prima facie* evils is *all things considered* evil must be less than $\left(\frac{1}{2} \times \frac{1}{2} \times \frac{1}{2}\right)$, and thus *less than* $\frac{1}{8}$.

Since each structure-description has an *a priori* probability of $\frac{1}{3}$, the probability that none of the three *prima facie* evils is an *all things considered* evil must be less than $\left\{ \left(\frac{1}{3} \times \frac{1}{2}\right) + \left(\frac{1}{3} \times \frac{1}{4}\right) + \left(\frac{1}{3} \times \frac{1}{8}\right) \right\} = \left(\frac{1}{6} + \frac{1}{12} + \frac{1}{24}\right) = \frac{7}{24}$.

Next, what is the probability if one assumes, instead, that all *state-descriptions* are equally likely? Using the terms 'A,' 'B,' and 'C' to refer to the three *prima facie* evils, one has the following five state-descriptions, each of which has an *a priori* probability of $\frac{1}{5}$:

State-description 1: A, B, and C are all related to the same morally significant property F.

State-description 2: A and B are related to the same morally significant property F, but C is related to a different morally significant property G.

State-description 3: A and C are related to the same morally significant property F, but B is related to a different morally significant property G.

State-description 4: B and C are related to the same morally significant property F, but A is related to a different morally significant property G.

State-description 5: A, B, and C are related to different morally significant properties, F, G, and H.

With state-descriptions, as with structure descriptions, there is always the 'counterbalancing failure' possibility that unknown rightmaking properties may not be sufficiently weighty to outweigh the known wrongmaking property. Taking that into account gives one the following results:

(1) The argument in the case of state-description 1 will be the same as with structure-description 1, so if state-description 1 obtains, the *a priori* probability that none of the *prima facie* evils are *all things considered* evils must be *less than* $\frac{1}{2}$.

(2) The arguments in the case of state-descriptions 2, 3, and 4 will be the same as with structure-description 2, so if state-description 2 obtains (and similarly for state-descriptions 3 and 4), the *a priori* probability that none of the *prima facie* evils are *all things considered* evils must be less than $\left(\frac{1}{2} \times \frac{1}{2}\right)$, and thus *less than* $\frac{1}{4}$.

(3) Finally, the argument will be the same in the case of state-description 5 as with structure-description 3, so the *a priori* probability that none of the *prima facie* evils are *all things considered* evils must be less than $\left(\frac{1}{2} \times \frac{1}{2} \times \frac{1}{2}\right)$, and thus *less than* $\frac{1}{8}$.

Since each state-description has an *a priori* probability of $\frac{1}{5}$, the probability that none of the three *prima facie* evils is an *all things considered* evil must be less than $\left\{ \left(\frac{1}{5}\times\frac{1}{2}\right)+\left(\frac{1}{5}\times\frac{1}{4}\right)+\left(\frac{1}{5}\times\frac{1}{4}\right)+\left(\frac{1}{5}\times\frac{1}{4}\right)+\left(\frac{1}{5}\times\frac{1}{8}\right) \right\} = \left(\frac{1}{10}+\frac{1}{20}+\frac{1}{20}+\frac{1}{20}+\frac{1}{40}\right) = \frac{4+2+2+2+1}{40} = \frac{11}{40}$.

On both a structure-description equiprobability assumption and on a state-description equiprobability assumption, the resulting probabilities are higher than they were, given the previous methods of calculating, with $\frac{7}{24}$ versus $\frac{1}{3+1} = \frac{1}{4} = \frac{6}{24}$ in the structure-description case, and $\frac{11}{40}$ versus $\left(\frac{1}{2}\right)^3 = \frac{1}{8} = \frac{5}{40}$ in the state-description case.

Structure-description calculations in this case always yield higher probabilities than state-description calculations. But while the structure-description result is slightly higher than with the $\frac{1}{N+1}$ rule that I had previously derived – when I failed to consider the possibility of a rightmaking property under which more than one, or even all, of the *prima facie* evils might fall – the difference is not very great. In particular, though I do not yet have a proof, because it is difficult to derive a general formula for the relevant probability given either a structure-description equiprobability assumption or a state-description equiprobability assumption, the calculations for a few cases – which are given in the Appendix – suggest that the probability is never greater than $\frac{1}{N}$.

Which of the two methods is right: a structure-description approach, or a state-description approach? I previously thought (Tooley and Plantinga 2008, 136–7) that a state-description equiprobability principle would, as Rudolf Carnap argued (1962, 564–5), have the consequence that one could never learn from experience. I have since realized, however, first, that Carnap's argument is unsound; secondly, that there is a very strong intuitive objection to a structure-description equiprobability principle; and, finally, that a state-description equiprobability assumption can be derived from four plausible equiprobability assumptions, including the two set out above in Section 4.4.

The upshot is that I now think that the correct version of the new approach is the one that employs a state-description equiprobability principle, where the latter principle, rather than being treated as fundamental, is derived from more fundamental equiprobability principles. What is important, however, is simply that regardless of which method is right, the probability that, given N *prima facie* evils, none of them is an *all things considered* evil, appears to be less than $\frac{1}{N}$, which means that in view of the enormous number of *prima facie* evils that the world contains, the probability that God exists, given those *prima facie* evils, is extremely low.

4.7 Is the Idea of Logical Probability Defensible?

Equiprobability-based arguments from evil involve the idea of logical probability. What about responding to such arguments, then, by contending that *the very idea* of logical probability is untenable?

To hold that the very idea of logical probability is completely untenable would be to hold that there are no propositions p and q, and no number k that is greater than zero and less than one, such that $\Pr(p/q) = k$. Confronted with that claim, one should ask about propositions of the following form:

(*) $\Pr(x$ is Q/x is P & (The proportion of things that are P that are Q is $\frac{m}{n}$)) $= \frac{m}{n}$.

If someone rejects this proposition, one can point out that Carnap (1947) and other philosophers who offered accounts of logical probability viewed the idea of logical probability as capturing something that it was rational to use as "a guide to life," and then one can ask the person what they would do in the following situation. There is a bag and a supply of red and green marbles, ten of which are to be put into the bag, and you get to specify how many of each color, the only constraint being that there must be at least one of each color. Suppose that you specify seven red marbles and three green ones. You must then play the following game. You decide on what odds you want to assign to the case that a marble that you yourself, without looking, draw from the bag will be red. Another person then decides whether you must bet that the marble you draw from the bag will be red, or, instead, that it will be green. If you are a rational person who has an aversion to losing money, can you select any odds other than seven to three that the marble that you draw from the bag will be red rather than green? But those are precisely the odds that correspond to the relevant instance of proposition (*). The logical probability given by (*) is thus a guide to what it is rational to do in the situation in question.

The conclusion, in short, is that while one may *say* that one totally rejects the idea of logical probability, what people take to be rational behavior in certain circumstances agrees completely with what it is rational to do according to the propositions specifying the relevant logical probability.

4.8 Objections to Equiprobability-Based Arguments from Evil?

What responses have there been to equiprobability-based arguments from evil? First of all, in my coauthored *Knowledge of God* debate volume (Plantinga and Tooley 2008), Plantinga raised objections to the version of the argument I set out there. In my response, I argued that, in view of two equiprobability principles – set out above in Section 4.4 – Plantinga's objections could be shown to be unsound.

What about subsequent responses? The answer, surprisingly, is that although it is now more than ten years on, not a single *journal* article criticizing equiprobability-based arguments from evil has appeared, based on both extensive internet searches and correspondence with several philosophers of religion, including skeptical theists. The only thing I found – aside from a blog post, no longer online – was one article in an anthology. Let us consider, then, those two responses.

4.8.1 Alexander Pruss

Alexander Pruss responded to my argument by advancing objections to Carnap's inductive logic. The most useful comments on that blog were by

Branden Fitelson, who said, first, "These objections to Carnapian inductive probability are not new," and secondly, after referring to a forthcoming article (2010) by Patrick Maher, "It is unfortunate that Tooley is using Carnap's earlier systems here, and not his later systems, which, as Maher explains, are much more interesting, (and also immune to the criticisms presented here)."

In the discussion that followed, Pruss focused on families of properties containing many members to raise objections to a formula Maher derives. Maher's derivation, however, was based on the assumption that the family of properties in question contained only two members (Maher 2010, 601–2). Pruss's objections, accordingly, were both beside the point and unfair.

4.8.2 Richard Otte

Much more interesting is Richard Otte's (2013) discussion, "A Carnapian Argument from Evil (Welcome Back, Skeptical Theism)." Here Otte offers objections both to my argument for the conclusion that the probability that God exists given a single *prima facie* evil is less than one-half, and also to part two of my argument, as set out previously (Tooley and Plantinga 2008 and Tooley 2012), according to which, given N *prima facie* evils, the probability that God exists must be less than $\frac{1}{N+1}$.

Part 1: The Case of a Single *Prima Facie* Evil

My argument for the first conclusion rested upon Equiprobability Principle 1, concerning families of properties. Otte does not offer any objections to this principle. Instead, he focuses upon a situation involving a finite collection of positive and negative integers, and the question is how probable it is that the sum of the integers in the collection is greater than zero. In response, Otte lists various symmetry principles, *none* of which are *general* symmetry principles, and *none* of which anyone setting out a theory of logical probability would think plausible.

The equiprobability principle needed to answer Otte's question is Equiprobability Principle 2 – The Interchange of Individuals – and if one applies that principle to Otte's example, it immediately follows that, for any number *n*, the *a priori* probability that *n* is in the collection is equal to the *a priori* probability that *–n* is in the collection. This, together with the probability that the sum of the numbers in the collection is equal to zero is either zero or infinitesimally close to zero, enables one to show that the *a priori* probability that the sum of the integers in the collection is greater than zero is either one-half or infinitesimally less than one-half.

Otte's commentary on his example, however, is as follows:

> Assigning an event probability of 1/2 is to make the strong claim that the
> event and its negation are equally likely, but, as in situations like this, we may
> have no reason to think that is the case. Because of this, withholding judg-
> ment is a safer response. Although going beyond our evidence and assigning
> the events equal probability may be rationally permissible, we certainly are
> not obligated to do so. (2013, 95)

Consider, however, a situation where a person is forced to bet on whether the
sum of the integers in Otte's example is greater than zero or less than zero,
where that person sets the odds, but another person then chooses which end of
the bet to take. What would one think if someone set the odds as one hundred to
one? Would one be in any doubt about which end of the bet to choose? Indeed,
would not one think that *any* specification of the odds other than fifty-fifty
would be irrational? If someone sincerely thought that choices other than fifty-
fifty would not be in any way irrational, it would seem that that person should be
perfectly willing to pick some other odds if forced to play the game. But would
anyone really do that?

Otte then goes on to consider a modified case where "the collection could
contain Aleph-Null, but not negative Aleph-Null" (2013, 95). He then says,

> Now suppose that the situation concerning rightmaking and wrongmaking
> properties is analogous to this second game: there can be infinitely strong
> rightmaking properties but no infinite wrongmaking properties. In this case,
> there is no symmetry between rightmaking and wrongmaking properties,
> because there are no unknown wrongmaking properties of infinite strength.
> But then Tooley's premise (2) should be rejected; we have no reason to think
> that relevant unknown wrongmaking properties are as probable as unknown
> rightmaking properties. (2013, 96)

But why would infinitely strong rightmaking properties be possible, yet not
infinitely strong wrongmaking properties? Consider, for example, the action of
creating an infinite number of innocent people who would be tormented forever.
Would not such an action have an infinitely strong wrongmaking property? But
then, if both the second-order property of being an infinitely strong rightmaking
property and the second-order property of being an infinitely strong wrongmaking
property can be instantiated and therefore exist, Equiprobability Principle 1
entails that the *a priori* probability that a property will possess the first of those
second-order properties is equal to the *a priori* probability that it will possess the
second of those second-order properties, thereby undercutting Otte's argument.

To sum up, then, the step in my argument concerned with a single *prima facie*
evil rests simply upon an equiprobability principle concerning families of
properties – a principle, moreover, that is essential to any theory of logical
probability, and against which Otte offers absolutely no argument. His strategy,

instead, involves trying to cast doubt on symmetry principles in general by focusing on the equiprobability principle that is concerned with the exchange of individual constants – Equiprobability Principle 2. But as we just saw, Otte's attempt to cast doubt on that principle forces him to make an extremely implausible claim about what it is not irrational to believe. The upshot is that Otte has failed to provide any good reason for rejecting my argument in the case of a single *prima facie* evil.

Part 2: The Case of Multiple *Prima Facie* Evils

Otte's discussion of the second step is more interesting, and his first and most important point is as follows:

> The central assumption of this argument is that God having a good reason to permit each evil is independent of God having a good reason to permit other evils. In other words, whether God has a good reason to permit a specific evil is independent of whether God has a good reason to permit any of the other evils, or even all of the other evils. We have good reason to reject this independence assumption; there being a good reason to permit one evil makes it more likely that there is a good reason to permit the other evils. (2013, 91)

Otte is right that, in *Knowledge of God* and "Inductive Logic and the Probability that God Exists: Farewell to Skeptical Theism," I overlooked both the possibility of goods that outweigh *multiple* evils that are necessary for the goods in question, and the possibility of greater evils that can be avoided only by allowing *multiple* lesser evils. As I indicated in Section 4.6.3, however, this is a point of which I had subsequently become aware, and which thus led to the two revised versions of my equiprobability arguments in the case of multiple evils.

Otte then attempts to support the idea that a great good can outweigh multiple evils, saying that "the value of a world that is regular and governed by physical laws is worth the cost of the suffering that various natural events bring about" (2013, 92). As I argued in Section 2.6, however, the idea that an appeal to the importance of laws of nature can serve to justify an omnipotent and omniscient person's not preventing various evils is untenable.

Otte next mentions the possibility of appealing to the "principle of indifference" to support assigning equal probabilities to all structure descriptions, and there he says, "Tooley needs to provide reason to assign equal probability to the structure descriptions; without this, his argument will be unconvincing" (2013, 92). My response here is, first, that the "principle of indifference" seems to me far too vague a principle to be used in formulating an inductive logic. Secondly, however, I agree with Otte that if one favors a structure-description equiprobability principle, one needs to offer some *justification* for that principle, since I do not think it is plausibly viewed as a fundamental principle. Thirdly and most important, as discussed above, I now think that there are decisive reasons for rejecting the view that structure-descriptions are equally probable – the one being that that principle, in contrast to a state-description equiprobability principle, cannot be derived from equiprobability principles that are plausibly viewed as fundamental; and the other being that a structure-description equiprobability principle leads to clearly unacceptable rules of succession: that advanced by Laplace, and, in a more general form, that advanced by Carnap in his *Logical Foundations of Probability* (1962, 567–568).

Finally, Otte claims that my argument "cannot be salvaged by appealing to the state description approach to inductive logic" (2013, 92) on the grounds that, as he mentioned earlier (2013, 88), Carnap had shown that the equiprobability state-description principle has the result that one cannot learn from experience. As noted earlier, however, not only is Carnap's argument unsound, his conclusion is false as well.

Summing up, then, the fundamental points are these. First, the right *starting point* for evidential arguments from evil is neither a state-description equiprobability principle nor a structure-description equiprobability principle – though the former principle is indeed correct and derivable from fundamental equiprobability principles. The right starting point is Equiprobability Principle 1 concerning families of properties, which I used in the case of a *single prima facie* evil. That principle is clearly sound, and the result is an argument to which Otte has no satisfactory response.

Secondly, I have formulated the argument concerning the probability that God exists given *multiple prima facie* evils in terms of both state-description and structure-description equiprobability principles. I believe, however, that a state-description equiprobability principle formulation is the correct one, and it can be proven, though I have not done so here, that a state-description equiprobability principle can be derived from equiprobability principles that are clearly fundamental, including the two set out in Section 4.4. Otte thought – and not unreasonably – that a state-description equiprobability principle cannot be correct, but his belief rested upon the unsound argument advanced by Rudolf Carnap. The upshot is that the new argument dealing with multiple evils that I set out in Section 4.6.3 is not open to any of Otte's objections.

Summary and Conclusions

The major division within arguments from evil against the existence of God, as well as, within limits, against deities that are less powerful, less knowledgeable, or morally less good, is between incompatibility arguments and evidential arguments. As regards the former, the main conclusions were, first, that they should be formulated using deontological concepts rather than axiological ones; secondly, that they should focus on specific types of evils – and most promisingly, on the suffering of sentient nonpersons; thirdly, that when this is done, crucial theodicies and defenses – in particular, soul-making, free will, and laws-of-nature ones – are rendered impotent; fourthly, that although it is often believed that skeptical theism provides a decisive answer to incompatibility arguments, one can formulate an incompatibility argument that shows that it is far from clear that this is so. The conclusion is thus that, at the very least, skeptical theists have much more work to do, since they need to show – as they have not done – that goods outside our ken can be logically connected in the required way to all of the evils found in the world.

As regards evidential arguments from evil, they come in four quite different forms: some employ a principle of universal instantial generalization; others involve only propositions – such as a version of Bayes' Theorem – that follow from a completely formal theory of probability; still others employ the principle of abduction; and finally, there are those based on fundamental equiprobability principles. Here I argued, first, that the first two types appear to be open to decisive objections; secondly, that the third type is based on a sound, albeit not fundamental, inductive principle, and that it can be so formulated that it cannot be refuted by an appeal to skeptical theism; and, finally, that the fourth type, which has been virtually ignored, rests upon completely sound equiprobability principles, and is, accordingly, an inductively sound argument from evil for the nonexistence of God, as well as of many lesser deities.

Appendix

Suppose one assumes that all structure-descriptions are equally likely. Then, as I mentioned, I have not yet found a formula specifying the probability, given N *prima facie* evils, that none of them are *all things considered* evils. Here, however, are results for a few initial cases, all of which assume that there are *relevant, unknown,* morally significant properties.

I shall represent structure-descriptions using expressions such as $\{x, y, z\}$, for example, which says that x *prima facie* evils have one particular unknown morally significant property, y *prima facie* evils have a different, unknown morally significant property, and z *prima facie* evils have yet another, distinct, unknown morally significant property.

Case 1: Two *Prima Facie* Evils

Here there are two relevant structure-descriptions – $\{2\}$ and $\{1, 1\}$ – each with a probability of $\frac{1}{2}$.

The probability that a given structure-description involves *only* rightmaking properties is as follows: For $\{2\}$: $\frac{1}{2}$; for $\{1, 1\}$: $\frac{1}{2} \times \frac{1}{2} = \frac{1}{4}$

Multiplying the probability of each structure-description by the probability that the structure-description involves only rightmaking properties gives:

$$\left[\left(\frac{1}{2} \times \frac{1}{2} = \frac{1}{4} \right) + \left(\frac{1}{2} \times \frac{1}{4} = \frac{1}{8} \right) \right] = \frac{2+1}{8} = \frac{3}{8}$$

Case 2: Three *Prima Facie* Evils

Here there are three relevant structure-descriptions – $\{3\}$, $\{2, 1\}$, and $\{1, 1, 1\}$ – each with a probability of $\frac{1}{3}$.

The probability that a given structure-description involves all rightmaking properties is as follows: For $\{3\}$: $\frac{1}{2}$; for $\{2, 1\}$: $\frac{1}{2} \times \frac{1}{2} = \frac{1}{4}$; for $\{1, 1, 1\}$: $\frac{1}{2} \times \frac{1}{2} \times \frac{1}{2} = \frac{1}{8}$.

Multiplying the probability of each structure-description by the probability that the structure-description involves only rightmaking properties gives:

$$\left[\left(\frac{1}{3} \times \frac{1}{2} = \frac{1}{6} \right) + \left(\frac{1}{3} \times \frac{1}{4} = \frac{1}{12} \right) + \left(\frac{1}{3} \times \frac{1}{8} = \frac{1}{24} \right) \right] = \frac{4+2+1}{24} = \frac{7}{24}$$

Case 3: Four *Prima Facie* Evils

Here there are five relevant structure-descriptions – $\{4\}$, $\{3,1\}$, $\{2,2\}$, $\{2,1,1\}$, and $\{1,1,1,1\}$ – each with a probability of $\frac{1}{5}$.

The probability that a given structure-description involves all rightmaking properties is as follows: For $\{4\}$: $\frac{1}{2}$; for $\{3,1\}$: $\frac{1}{2} \times \frac{1}{2} = \frac{1}{4}$; for $\{2,2\}$: $\frac{1}{2} \times \frac{1}{2} = \frac{1}{4}$; for $\{2,1,1\}$: $\frac{1}{2} \times \frac{1}{2} \times \frac{1}{2} = \frac{1}{8}$; for $\{1,1,1,1\}$: $\frac{1}{2} \times \frac{1}{2} \times \frac{1}{2} \times \frac{1}{2} = \frac{1}{16}$.

Multiplying the probability of each structure-description by the probability that the structure-description involves only rightmaking properties gives:

$$\left[\left(\frac{1}{5} \times \frac{1}{2} = \frac{1}{10}\right) + \left(\frac{1}{5} \times \frac{1}{4} = \frac{1}{20}\right) + \left(\frac{1}{5} \times \frac{1}{4} = \frac{1}{20}\right) + \left(\frac{1}{5} \times \frac{1}{8} = \frac{1}{40}\right)\right.$$
$$\left.+ \left(\frac{1}{5} \times \frac{1}{16} = \frac{1}{80}\right)\right] = \frac{8+4+4+2+1}{80} = \frac{19}{80}$$

Case 4: Five *Prima Facie* Evils

Here there are seven relevant structure-descriptions – $\{5\}$, $\{4,1\}$, $\{3,2\}$, $\{3,1,1\}$, $\{2,2,1\}$, $\{2,1,1,1\}$, and $\{1,1,1,1,1\}$ – each with a probability of $\frac{1}{7}$.

The probability that a given structure description involves all rightmaking properties is as follows: For $\{5\}$: $\frac{1}{2}$; for $\{4,1\}$: $\frac{1}{2} \times \frac{1}{2} = \frac{1}{4}$; for $\{3,2\}$: $\frac{1}{2} \times \frac{1}{2} = \frac{1}{4}$; for $\{3,1,1\}$: $\frac{1}{2} \times \frac{1}{2} \times \frac{1}{2} = \frac{1}{8}$; for $\{2,2,1\}$: $\frac{1}{2} \times \frac{1}{2} \times \frac{1}{2} = \frac{1}{8}$; for $\{2,1,1,1\}$: $\frac{1}{2} \times \frac{1}{2} \times \frac{1}{2} \times \frac{1}{2} = \frac{1}{16}$; for $\{1,1,1,1,1\}$: $\frac{1}{2} \times \frac{1}{2} \times \frac{1}{2} \times \frac{1}{2} \times \frac{1}{2} = \frac{1}{32}$.

Multiplying the probability of each structure-description by the probability that the structure-description involves only rightmaking properties gives:

$$\left[\left(\frac{1}{7} \times \frac{1}{2} = \frac{1}{14}\right) + \left(\frac{1}{7} \times \frac{1}{4} = \frac{1}{28}\right) + \left(\frac{1}{7} \times \frac{1}{4} = \frac{1}{28}\right) + \left(\frac{1}{7} \times \frac{1}{8} = \frac{1}{56}\right)\right.$$
$$\left.+ \left(\frac{1}{7} \times \frac{1}{8} = \frac{1}{56}\right) + \left(\frac{1}{7} \times \frac{1}{16} = \frac{1}{112}\right) + \left(\frac{1}{7} \times \frac{1}{32} = \frac{1}{224}\right)\right]$$
$$= \frac{16+8+8+4+4+2+1}{224} = \frac{43}{224}$$

The previous method of calculating using the structure-descriptions equi-probability principle led to the result that given N *prima facie* evils, the probability that none of them was an *all things considered* evil was less than $\frac{1}{N+1}$. The

Appendix

new method generates values that are greater than $\frac{1}{N+1}$, as one can see from the following table:

Table of Comparisons

Case	1	2	3	4
Number N of Evils	2	3	4	5
Probability Is Equal to	$\frac{3}{8} = \frac{1260}{3360}$	$\frac{7}{24} = \frac{980}{3360}$	$\frac{19}{80} = \frac{798}{3360}$	$\frac{43}{224} = \frac{645}{3360}$
Value of $\frac{1}{N}$	$\frac{1}{2} = \frac{1680}{3360}$	$\frac{1}{3} = \frac{1120}{3360}$	$\frac{1}{4} = \frac{840}{3360}$	$\frac{1}{5} = \frac{672}{3360}$
Value of $\frac{1}{N+1}$	$\frac{1}{3} = \frac{1120}{3360}$	$\frac{1}{4} = \frac{840}{3360}$	$\frac{1}{5} = \frac{672}{3360}$	$\frac{1}{6} = \frac{560}{3360}$
Ratio of Probability to $\frac{1}{N}$	$\frac{3}{4} = \frac{840}{1120}$	$\frac{7}{8} = \frac{980}{1120}$	$\frac{19}{20} = \frac{1064}{1120}$	$\frac{215}{224} = \frac{1075}{1120}$

One can also see, however, that in the cases considered, given N *prima facie* evils, the probability that none of them is an *all things considered* evil is less than $\frac{1}{N}$. In the absence of a general formula one cannot be confident that this will be so as N gets larger, but the last line in the above table does suggest that as N increases, the probability in question approaches a limit of $\frac{1}{N}$. Since $\frac{1}{N}$ gets closer and close to $\frac{1}{N+1}$ as N increases, this means that the probability gets squeezed between $\frac{1}{N}$ and $\frac{1}{N+1}$ as N increases.

References

Benson H., et al. (2006) "Study of the Therapeutic Effects of Intercessory Prayer (STEP) in Cardiac Bypass Patients: A Multicenter Randomized Trial of Uncertainty and Certainty of Receiving Intercessory Prayer," *American Heart Journal* **151/4**, 934–42.

Bergmann, Michael (2001) "Skeptical Theism and Rowe's New Evidential Argument from Evil," *Nous* **35**, 278–96.

(2009) "Skeptical Theism and the Problem of Evil." In Thomas Flint and Michael Rea, (eds.), *Oxford Handbook of Philosophical Theology*, Oxford: Oxford University Press, pp. 374–99.

Best, Ben (2018) *The Anatomical Basis of Mind*, Chapter 6, "Basic Cerebral Cortex Function Other than Vision," Section IV, Available from www .benbest.com/science/anatmind/anatmd6.html (accessed May 9, 2019).

Carnap, Rudolf (1947) "Probability as a Guide in Life," *Journal of Philosophy* **44/6**, 141–8.

(1962) *Logical Foundations of Probability*, Second Edition, Chicago: The University of Chicago Press.

Carruthers, Peter (2018) "The Problem of Animal Consciousness," *Proceedings of the American Philosophical Association* **92**, 179–205.

Dougherty, Trent (2011) "Recent Work on the Problem of Evil," *Analysis* 71/3, 560–73.

(2012) "Reconsidering the Parent Analogy – Further Work for Skeptical Theists," *International Journal for Philosophy of Religion* **72/1**, 17–25.

(2013) "Reflections on Explanation and Draper's Argument." In Justin P. McBrayer and Daniel Howard-Snyder, (eds.), *The Blackwell Companion to the Problem of Evil*, Malden: Wiley Blackwell, 2013, pp. 75–82.

(2014) *The Problem of Animal Pain: A Theodicy for All Creatures Great and Small*, New York & Basingstoke: Palgrave MacMillan.

(2016) "Skeptical Theism," *The Stanford Encyclopedia of Philosophy* (Winter 2016 Edition), Edward N. Zalta (ed.). Available from https://plato.stanford .edu/archives/win192016/entries/skeptical-theism/ (accessed April 12, 2019).

Dougherty, Trent, and McBrayer, Justin P. (2014) *Skeptical Theism: New Essays*, New York: Oxford University Press.

Draper, Paul (1989) "Pain and Pleasure: An Evidential Problem for Theists," *Noûs* **23**, 331–350. Reprinted in Howard-Snyder, Daniel (ed.), *The*

Evidential Argument from Evil, Bloomington: Indiana University Press, 1996, pp. 12–29.

(2013) "Humean Arguments from Evil." In Justin P. McBrayer and Daniel Howard-Snyder, (eds.), *The Blackwell Companion to the Problem of Evil,* Malden: Wiley Blackwell, pp. 67–75.

Hick, John (1966) *Evil and the God of Love,* New York: Harper and Rowe, revised edition 1978.

Howard-Snyder, Daniel, (ed.) (1996) *The Evidential Argument from Evil,* Bloomington and Indianapolis: Indiana University Press.

(2009) "Epistemic Humility, Arguments from Evil, and Moral Skepticism." In Jonathan Kvanig (ed.), *Oxford Studies in Philosophy of Religion*, vol. 2, Oxford: Oxford University Press, pp. 17–57.

(2015). "How Not to Render an Explanatory Version of the Evidential Argument from Evil Immune to Skeptical Theism," *International Journal for Philosophy of Religion*, 78:277–284.

Hudson, Hud (2001) *A Materialist Metaphysics of the Human Person*, Ithaca and New York: Cornell University Press.

Hume, David (1779) *Dialogues Concerning Natural Religion.* Reprinted (1947), with an introduction by Norman Kemp Smith, New York: Bobbs Merrill.

Kaufman, Whitley (2005) "Karma, Rebirth, and the Problem of Evil," *Philosophy East and West* **55/1**, 15–32.

Keynes, John Maynard (1921) *A Treatise on Probability*, London and New York, Macmillan and Company.

Kieffer, Brigitte (2007) "How Does the Opioid System Control Pain, Reward and Addictive Behavior?" *20th European College of Neuropsychopharmacology Congress on Neuropsychopharmacology*, Vienna, Austria.

Krucoff M. W. et al. (2005) "Music, Imagery, Touch, and Prayer as Adjuncts to Interventional Cardiac Care: The Monitoring and Actualisation of Noetic Trainings (MANTRA) II Randomised Study," *Lancet* **366** (9481), 211–17.

Laplace, Pierre Simon de (1812) *Théorie analytique de probabilities*, Paris.

Leibniz, Gottfried Wilhelm (1714) *The Monadology*, translated by Jonathan Bennett, www.earlymoderntexts.com/assets/pdfs/leibniz1714b.pdf (accessed November 12, 2018).

Maher, Patrick (2010) "Explication of Inductive Probability," *Journal of Philosophical Logic* **39/6**, 593–616.

McBrayer, Justin P. and Howard-Snyder, Daniel (eds.) (2013) *The Blackwell Companion to the Problem of Evil*, Malden: Wiley Blackwell.

Morriston, Wes (2014) "Skeptical Demonism: A Failed Response to a Humean Challenge." In Trent Dougherty, and Justin P. McBrayer, (eds.), *Skeptical Theism: New Essays*, Oxford: Oxford University Press, pp. 209–220.

Murray, Michael (2008) *Nature Red in Tooth and Claw: Theism and the Problem of Animal Suffering*, Oxford: Oxford University Press.

Nickell, Joe (1993) *Looking for a Miracle*, Amherst, NY: Prometheus Books.

Nolen, William A. (1974) *Healing: A Doctor in Search of a Miracle*, New York: Random House Inc.

Otte, Richard (2013) "A Carnapian Argument from Evil (Welcome Back, Skeptical Theism)." In Justin P. McBrayer and Daniel Howard-Snyder, (eds.), *The Blackwell Companion to the Problem of Evil*, Malden: Wiley Blackwell, 2013, pp. 83–97.

Otto, Rudolf (1958) *The Idea of the Holy*, translated by John W. Harvey, New York: Oxford University Press.

Peirce, C. S. (1883) "A Theory of Probable Inference," reprinted in *Collected Papers*, Charles Hartshorne and Paul Weiss (eds.), Cambridge, MA: Harvard University Press, Vol. II (1932), pp. 470f.

Plantinga, Alvin (1974a) *God, Freedom, and Evil*, New York: Harper and Row.

(1974b) *The Nature of Necessity*, Oxford: Clarendon Press.

(1998) "Degenerate Evidence and Rowe's New Evidential Argument from Evil," *Noûs* **32/4**, 531–44.

(2000) *Warranted Christian Belief*, New York: Oxford University Press.

Plantinga, Alvin and Michael Tooley (2008) *Knowledge of God*, Oxford: Blackwell Publishing.

Pruss, Alexander (2010) Tooley's Use of Carnap's Probability Measure. Originally posted on http://prosblogion.ektopos.com/archives/2010/02/tooleys-use-of.html but apparently no longer available online.

Randi, James (1987) *The Faith Healers*, Buffalo, New York: Prometheus Books.

Robison, Andrew Cliffe (1962) *Mysticism and Philosophy: The Problem of Cognitive Value*, Senior Thesis in the Department of Religion, Princeton University.

(1973) *Religious Experience and Justified Religious Belief*, PhD Dissertation in the Department of Philosophy, Princeton University.

(1975) "Religious Experience." In Malcolm L. Diamond and Thomas V. Litzenburg, Jr. (eds.), *The Logic of God: Theology and Verification*, Indianapolis: The Bobbs-Merrill Company, Inc, pp. 409–32.

Rose, Louis (1968) *Faith Healing*, London: Victor Gollancz.

Rowe, William L. (1979) "The Problem of Evil and Some Varieties of Atheism," *American Philosophical Quarterly* **16/4**, 335–41

(1988) "Evil and Theodicy," *Philosophical Topics* **16/2**, 119–32.

(1991) "Ruminations about Evil," *Philosophical Perspectives* **5**, 69–88.

(1996) "The Evidential Argument from Evil: A Second Look." In Daniel Howard-Snyder (ed.), *The Evidential Argument from Evil*, Bloomington: Indiana University Press, 262–85.

(1998) "Reply to Plantinga," *Noûs*, **32/4**, 545–52.

(2001) "Skeptical Theism: A Response to Bergmann," *Noûs* **35/2**, 297–303.

(2006). "Friendly Atheism, Skeptical Theism, and the Problem of Evil," *International Journal for Philosophy of Religion* **59/2**: 79–92.

Russell, Bruce, and Wykstra, Stephen (1988) "The 'Inductive' Problem of Evil: A Dialogue," *Philosophical Topics* **16/2**, 133–60.

Swinburne, Richard (1996) "Some Major Strands of Theodicy." In Daniel Howard-Snyder, (ed.), *The Evidential Argument from Evil*, Bloomington: Indiana University Press, 1996, pp. 30–48.

(1998) *Providence and the Problem of Evil*, Oxford: Oxford University Press.

Tomberlin, James E. (ed.) (1991) *Philosophical Perspectives 5: Philosophy of Religion*, Atascadero, CA: Ridgeview Publishing.

Tooley, Michael (1977) "The Nature of Laws," *Canadian Journal of Philosophy*, **7/4**, 667–98.

(1981) "Plantinga's Defence of the Ontological Argument," *Mind* **90**, 422–7.

(1987) *Causation: A Realist Approach*, Oxford: Oxford University Press.

(2009) "A Philosophical Journey," *Proceedings and Addresses of the American Philosophical Association* **83/2**, 97–115.

(2011) "Hume and the Problem of Evil." In Jeffrey J. Jordan, (ed.), *Philosophy of Religion: The Key Thinkers*, London and New York, Continuum, pp. 159–86.

(2012) "Inductive Logic and the Probability that God Exists: Farewell to Skeptical Theism." In Jake Chandler, and Victoria S. Harrison, (ed.), *Probability in the Philosophy of Religion*, Oxford, Oxford University Press, pp. 144–64.

(2016) "The Problem of Evil," *The Stanford Encyclopedia of Philosophy* (Winter 2016 Edition), Edward N. Zalta (ed.), https://plato.stanford.edu/archives/win2016/entries/evil/

Tooley, Michael, and Plantinga, Alvin (2008) *Knowledge of God*, Oxford: Blackwell Publishing.

van Inwagen, Peter (1978) "The Possibility of Resurrection," *International Journal for Philosophy of Religion* **9/2**, 114–21.

(1991) "The Problem of Evil, the Problem of Air, and the Problem of Silence." In James E. Tomberlin, (ed.), *Philosophical Perspectives, 5, Philosophy of Religion, 1991*, pp. 135–165.

(2006) *The Problem of Evil*, Oxford: Oxford University Press.

West, D. J. (1957) *Eleven Lourdes Miracles*, London: Gerald Duckworth and Company.

White, Andrew D. (1896) *A History of the Warfare of Science with Theology within Christendom*, Buffalo, New York: Prometheus Books, 1993.

Wittgenstein, Ludwig (1922) *Tractatus Logico-Philosophicus*, with an introduction by Bertrand Russell. Translated by D. F. Pears and B. F. McGuiness, London, Routledge and Kegan Paul, 1961.

Wykstra, Stephen J. (1984) "The Humean Obstacle to Evidential Arguments from Suffering: On Avoiding the Evils of 'Appearance'," *International Journal for Philosophy of Religion* **16/2**, 73–93.

(1996) "Rowe's Noseeum Arguments from Evil." In Daniel Howard-Snyder, (ed.), *The Evidential Argument from Evil*, Bloomington and Indianapolis: Indiana University Press, pp. 126–50.

Cambridge Elements

Philosophy of Religion

Yujin Nagasawa
University of Birmingham
Yujin Nagasawa is Professor of Philosophy and Co-Director of the John Hick Centre for
Philosophy of Religion at the University of Birmingham. He is currently President of the
British Society for the Philosophy of Religion. He is a member of the Editorial Board of
Religious Studies, the *International Journal for Philosophy of Religion* and *Philosophy
Compass*.

About the Series
This Cambridge Elements series provides concise and structured introductions to all the
central topics in the philosophy of religion. It offers balanced, comprehensive coverage
of multiple perspectives in the philosophy of religion. Contributors to the series are
cutting-edge researchers who approach central issues in the philosophy of religion. Each
provides a reliable resource for academic readers and develops new ideas and
arguments from a unique viewpoint.

Cambridge Elements ≡

Philosophy of Religion

Printed in the United States
By Bookmasters